SMART COOKIES

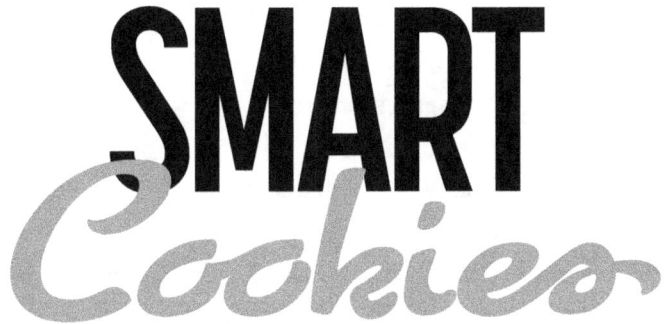

HOW HOME COOKS BECAME FINALISTS IN THE PILLSBURY BAKE-OFF® CONTEST

By Mary Beth Protomastro

Springform Press LLC
New York

Copyright © 2017 by Mary Beth Protomastro

Springform Press LLC
P.O. Box 230675
New York, NY 10023-0675
springformpress.com

All rights reserved. No part of this publication may be reproduced, distributed, or transmitted in any form or by any means, including photocopying, recording, or other electronic or mechanical methods, without the prior written permission of the publisher, except in the case of brief quotations.

Pillsbury, Bake-Off, and Doughboy are registered trademarks of General Mills and/or its affiliates, used with permission. The views and opinions expressed in this book are solely those of the author and do not reflect the official policies or views of General Mills.

Mention of specific companies, organizations, or authorities in this book does not imply endorsement by the author or the publisher, nor does mention of specific companies, organizations, or authorities imply that they endorse this book, the author, or the publisher.

Cover photograph by Victor Torres/Stocksy
Back cover photograph courtesy of General Mills
Cover and interior design by Danielle Foster

ISBN: 978-0-9989935-0-8

Printed in the United States of America

CONTENTS

Introduction   1

1   Perseverance Pays Off   9
It takes a special kind of tenacity to enter the Pillsbury Bake-Off Contest for decades in the hope of getting in. How Marie Sheppard, Mary Hawkes, Heidi Givler, and Marie Bruno persisted—and ended their dry spells.

2   Batting a Thousand   27
Yes, it is possible to beat the odds and become a finalist every time you enter. Arlene Erlbach, Marie Valdes, and Victoria Croce have proved it.

3   Resilience, Their Secret Ingredient   41
Depression. Cancer. Grief. How the ability to bounce back from adversity made finalists out of Shana Butler, Michele Kusma, Carole Resnick, Brenda Watts, and Linda Drumm.

CONTENTS

4 Three Times and Out   71

Becoming a finalist for the maximum three times is a rare achievement. What home cooks can learn from Cathy Wiechert, Laureen Pittman, and Pamela Shank.

5 Last Dance With the Doughboy   85

Two-time finalists have just one more chance to compete in the Bake-Off Contest, under current rules. Taking stock with Kim Van Dunk, JoAnn Belack, Kellie White, Amy Siegel, Lise Sullivan Ode, and Sindee Morgan.

6 A First Taste of the Bake-Off Contest   113

Compete once and you're hooked. Lesley Pew, Kim Rollings, and Becky Pifer tell what it was like to become a first-time finalist.

7 Winners' Circle   125

Beth Royals, Christina Verrelli, and Anna Ginsberg, all winners of the million-dollar grand prize, discuss their strategies and experiences.

Appendixes

A. Pillsbury Bake-Off Contest Winners   141

B. Bake-Off Recipes That Repurposed Pillsbury Products   145

C. Three Award-Winning Recipes From the 47th Pillsbury Bake-Off Contest   153

D. Further Reading   157

Acknowledgments

Heartfelt thanks to everyone who helped make *Smart Cookies* a reality. Nanette Varian deserves a grand prize of her own for her enthusiasm, support, and guidance, right from the beginning; now I know why all the writers at *More* magazine loved her. I'm grateful also to copy editor Dorothy Irwin, designer Danielle Foster, researcher Molly M. Ginty, and everyone else who helped in one way or another, especially Christa Bundt of General Mills, Mary Flower, Sheila Buff, and Nancy Protomastro. Special thanks to all the finalists who were interviewed for *Smart Cookies;* their encouragement and willingness to share their experiences exemplify the Pillsbury Bake-Off Contest spirit.

Introduction

While visiting my parents at their New Jersey home in January 2012, I came across an article in their local newspaper, the Bergen *Record:* TWO CLIFTON WOMEN LOOK TO TAKE THE $1M CAKE AT BAKE-OFF. Those two women were among 100 finalists vying for a million dollars in the 45th Pillsbury Bake-Off Contest, to be held that March, the article said. Amy Siegel would be competing with her Strawberry Swirl–Peanut Butter–Brownie Cupcakes, and Kathy Matulewicz with her Coconut-Almond Doughnut Pop-ems; both recipes appeared with the article.

My life hasn't been the same since.

The Pillsbury Bake-Off Contest! I hadn't thought of it in ages, probably not since I'd seen the competition on TV as a teenager in the 1970s. After I read the article, I thought, Why am I not doing that? I love to bake—cakes, cupcakes, cookies, cobblers, muffins. Amy's and Kathy's recipes were both impressive, but Amy's fascinated me. Choosing ingredients from prescribed lists, Amy made cupcakes from brownie mix, filled them with a peanut butter–sweetened condensed milk mixture, and topped them with a strawberry–cream cheese frosting. They sounded like a mash-up of two sandwiches I enjoyed as a kid, PB&J and cream cheese and jelly, only with chocolate cake instead of bread. And devising this recipe gave her a 1-in-100 chance of winning a million dollars!

Over the next two months, I visited the Pillsbury website (pillsbury.com) to see the other recipes in the running. Then, on her TV show, Martha Stewart announced the winner: Christina Verrelli, who had entered a standout dessert called Pumpkin Ravioli With Salted Caramel Whipped Cream. I'll never forget the excitement coming from my television screen—the smiles, the hugs, the confetti, against a backdrop of baked goods and cooked dishes. If the Bake-Off Contest was all about food, fun, and a chance to win money, I had to enter it myself.

When the next Contest opened, in January 2013, I reviewed the lists of eligible products (participants had to choose one from list A and one from list B, or two from list A). And then for weeks I worked to perfect my Chocolate Hazelnut Torte, which consisted of a sponge cake brushed with hazelnut simple syrup, filled with mousse, topped with ganache, and decorated with whipped cream. It was heavenly. I created a second entry along those lines, but cupcake size.

Alas, my recipes didn't make it in. Why not? The answer, I figured, must lie in the ones that did. And so I studied those recipes, this time paying attention to how they were made, not just what they made.

I already knew that the recipes had to be original—no easy feat—but there were a few things I'd missed. First, when I carefully read the finalists' recipe instructions, I saw that these home cooks had devised simple methods that packed a big punch. My recipes were far too complicated. That point became crystal clear

INTRODUCTION

when I compared my Chocolate Hazelnut Torte with Marie Bruno's Decadent Chocolate Hazelnut Tart, which, as Marie notes on page 22, was "tasty and deceptively easy to make."

Second, many of the finalists had used the eligible products more creatively than I had. Brenda Watts had taken Pillsbury refrigerated sugar cookie dough, Jif Chocolate Hazelnut Spread, and other ingredients and turned them into Chocolate Cherry Soufflé Cupcakes. Michele Kusma had used the same cookie dough to make Blueberry Sour Cream Pancakes. Lise Sullivan Ode's German Chocolate Doughnuts started out as Pillsbury Grands! Flaky Layers refrigerated Honey Butter biscuits. (See page 145 for a list of Bake-Off recipes in which finalists have repurposed Pillsbury products.)

Third, there was nothing out of the ordinary about my tortes. Even though my recipes were original, there were plenty like them. By contrast, consider Kim Van Dunk's finalist entry: She threaded Pillsbury refrigerated breadsticks around meatballs on skewers to make Meatball and Breadstick Sub Skewers, a novel idea in 2013. Thanks to Kim's ingenuity, home cooks around the country are now making and passing along this clever recipe.

Reviewing the methods used in the Contest 46 recipes was eye-opening. Through their recipes, the finalists showed me how much fun it was to be creative with food. It became hard to stop thinking of new recipes! This time, I didn't just decide to enter the next Contest; I promised myself that I would try my hardest to become a finalist.

I kept my promise, and in June 2014 the 47th Pillsbury Bake-Off Contest accepted my easy recipe for Caprese Corn Cakes, made with Pillsbury refrigerated sugar cookie dough. When I Googled "Caprese Corn Cakes" back then, I didn't get a single hit. The dish was a twist on a twist: I modeled it on MozzArepas, sweet corn pancakes sandwiched with mozzarella, which are themselves modeled on arepas, Colombian cornmeal cakes. I was familiar with MozzArepas because they're sold at street fairs in New York City, where I live. But no amount of MozzArepa eating would have inspired my dish had I not carefully read the recipes of my Bake-Off forebears. They showed me the way.

Shortly after Pillsbury released the names of the finalists, in the summer of 2014, Kim Van Dunk invited me to join a Facebook group she'd started for the 100 competitors in that year's Contest. That's how I first got to know my fellow finalists, who proved to be a smart, adventurous bunch whose sense of humor seemed to mesh with mine. I remember sitting in my cubicle at *More* magazine, where I was the copy chief, trying to stifle my laughter over their comments about an unusual photograph that had accompanied an article about the upcoming Bake-Off Contest. One of the two women in the photo was wearing a bustier, which had the group joking that Pillsbury must have decided to switch out the aprons that year.

Through the Facebook group, I became acquainted with Amy Siegel, whose brownie cupcakes had gotten me started on this adventure in January 2012. This time she was competing with a savory dish, Sesame Mini Pitas With Roasted Red Pepper Tapenade. It turned out that Amy and I were scheduled to travel to the Bake-Off Contest, held that year in Nashville, on the same flight out of Newark Liberty International Airport. In fact, my assigned seat was right behind Amy's! We arranged to meet in the airport before the flight for a chat. I couldn't wait to have a live conversation with a previous finalist—someone who knew the ins and outs of

INTRODUCTION

the event that had captured my fascination for nearly three years. Amy answered all my questions so intelligently and reasonably and warmly that I thought, If the other finalists are anything like Amy, I'm going to have a great time in Nashville.

One thing became clear as I got to know my fellow finalists: They were knowledgeable about baking (or cooking, or both) from scratch. If you don't know how the essential components work—eggs, baking powder, liquids—how can you take a prepared product and turn it into something else? At least three times in this book you'll see finalists talking about working "backwards" with a prepared product. As Laureen Pittman says on page 77, "Instead of thinking, What could I do with a biscuit? I thought of it as, It's really just flour. Check the ingredients and think about what you could do with those instead of a biscuit."

Smart cookies, these finalists—and not just the ones I competed with, but all the Bake-Off finalists I've gotten to know. As I learned in interviewing them, they're remarkable in many ways: Some are blessed with perseverance, some with resilience, some with a cleverness I can only wish for. All are optimists, having beaten long odds to get into the Contest.

Here are the stories of 27 people whose enthusiasm and affection for the Pillsbury Bake-Off Contest have continued long since their competitions ended. They first inspired me with their tales of how they became Bake-Off finalists; I now look to them also as role models for pursuing a goal, for picking myself up after a hardship, and for making room in my life for a hobby that brings joy and friendship.

Facts About the Pillsbury Bake-Off Contest

- The Pillsbury Company started the Pillsbury Bake-Off Contest in 1949, calling it the Grand National Recipe and Baking Contest. The competition has had several names over the years (in *Smart Cookies*, it's consistently called the Pillsbury Bake-Off Contest to prevent confusion).

- The grand prize was initially $25,000. It grew to $40,000 in 1980, to $50,000 in 1992, and to $1 million in 1996.

- The Contest rules can and do change from one competition to the next. Qualifying ingredients, preparation time, awards, eligibility requirements for participants—every aspect of the Contest is subject to change, including the grand prize.

- In the early competitions, one ingredient was required for entry: a half cup of Pillsbury Best flour. Baked goods made from scratch accounted for nearly all the winning entries in the first two decades.

- In 1968, Pillsbury created two new categories, for baking mixes and refrigerated dough.

- The first year a recipe made with refrigerated dough won the grand prize was 1969. The recipe: Magic Marshmallow Crescent Puffs.

- The entries for each competition, which number in the tens of thousands, are first evaluated by an independent judging agency. It removes the contestants' identifying information, weeds out entries that don't meet the requirements, and sends the 400 or so most appealing entries to the Pillsbury kitchens. The home economists there test and evaluate the recipes and research them for originality before whittling the number down to 100.

INTRODUCTION

- All 100 finalists compete at the same time, in mini kitchens set up in a hotel ballroom. Pillsbury assembles 102 mini kitchens; two are spares in case of technical problems, such as a malfunctioning range.

- The judges who choose the award winners from the 100 finalists don't work for Pillsbury. Most are food editors and writers who work for print or online publications.

- Guests and hosts over the years have included Eleanor Roosevelt, Ronald Reagan, Marie Osmond, Joy Behar, and Padma Lakshmi.

- Women predominate in the competition; in 2014, of the 100 finalists, 95 were women.

- There was no age requirement for participants in the first Pillsbury Bake-Off Contest. From 1950 to 2004, the minimum age varied from 10 to 13 (though in the early '50s, males had to be 20 or older). Since 2005, the minimum age has been 18.

- Beginning in 1979, Bake-Off finalists have been limited to three competitions.

- Like Major League Baseball, the Pillsbury Bake-Off Contest has a Hall of Fame, instituted in 1999 to recognize the most popular recipes submitted by finalists. Among the 14 Hall of Famers are Broccoli-Cauliflower Tetrazzini, French Silk Chocolate Pie, Ham and Cheese Crescent Snacks, Peanut Blossoms, and Tunnel of Fudge Cake.

- Since 2001, the competition has been owned by General Mills, which also owns the Pillsbury refrigerated dough products. General Mills owns the Pillsbury brand but licenses it to Smucker's for shelf-stable products such as flour and dry baking mixes.

About the Advice in This Book

Following the advice in this book does not guarantee that you'll become a finalist in the Pillsbury Bake-Off Contest, for a number of reasons. Among them: The Contest receives tens of thousands of entries, and the rules always change. The comments by the finalists and the author reflect their interpretations of the rules and the reasons their recipes were accepted, as well as their personalities and experiences.

CHAPTER 1

Perseverance Pays Off

WHAT DOES IT TAKE to enter the Pillsbury Bake-Off Contest for 20 years or more in the hope of getting in for the first time? Perseverance, optimism, and, of course, an abiding interest in cooking or baking. Marie Sheppard, Mary Hawkes, Heidi Givler, and Marie Bruno have those qualities in spades.

Marie Sheppard
Chicago

CONTEST 46 *Blueberry Cinnamon Roll Coffee Cake*
CONTEST 47 *Lemon-Broccoli Risotto Rounds*

As a four-year-old, Marie Sheppard would be awakened by her maternal grandmother every weekday morning after her parents left for work. Then their ritual would begin: Grandma would prepare bread dough and break off a small piece for young Marie, who would stand on a chair so she could reach the countertop and mimic her grandmother's kneading. "It was just some of the best times I can remember," Sheppard says, "and ever since then, I've always liked to cook."

But even for people who have enjoyed cooking from a young age, acceptance into the Pillsbury Bake-Off Contest can be elusive. Sheppard, for example, entered it regularly for 20 years—from 1993 to 2013—before she became a finalist. Her circuitous route to the competition began by chance, after she left her teaching job because of illness, which turned out to be ulcerative colitis. "I had a long recovery," she says, "so I would lie around, and one day I was reading *Good Housekeeping* and stumbled upon a contest the magazine was doing in tandem with Newman's Own. The finalists would get money for charity—you know, Paul Newman was always so philanthropic." Sheppard had lost a dear friend to AIDS, "and I thought if I could get this money to give to the AIDS clinic here in Chicago, it would make me feel really good," she says. Her Spinach, Turkey, and Apple Salad recipe made it to the final round, earning Sheppard $10,000 for the clinic and a trip to New York City to meet Newman and the Newman's Own staff.

"We had limos taking us all over New York, fantastic restaurants, tickets to see Regis and Kathie Lee," says Sheppard, noting that sponsor companies were especially generous with contest finalists back then. "I thought, I like this, so I started entering [other cooking contests], and I thought of the Pillsbury Bake-Off. That's just the gold standard of all recipe contests. So I kept entering and entering"—she submitted an average of five recipes each time—"and nothing. But I wasn't discouraged." Things started looking up in 2009, when she was named a semifinalist for the 2010 Contest, but she didn't receive enough online votes to become a finalist. The same thing happened two years later. After she became a semifinalist in the 2013 Contest, which also involved voting, "I was so sure I wasn't going to win that I booked a trip to New York for a long weekend during the Bake-Off," says Sheppard, a lifelong Chicagoan. But this time she received enough votes, and her 20-year wait was over. "I couldn't believe it. I ran around my house screaming," she says. And she canceled the trip to New York.

The recipe that won Sheppard her first spot in the competition was Blueberry Cinnamon Roll Coffee Cake, which she entered as Blueberry Cinnamon Roll Babka Bake. "They changed the name," she says. "Maybe people were not familiar with the term *babka*." The preparation entails enveloping a mixture of blueberries, blueberry preserves, and lemon zest in flattened cinnamon rolls, which are then arranged, spoke-like, in a tart pan. The cinnamon appealed to Sheppard, who enjoys cooking with spices. "I thought, Blueberries and spice—what's not to like?" She says she developed the recipe as "kind of a brunch thing. I like to have people over for brunch because it's a little more relaxed and it can go into the afternoon if you want. And what better way to walk into someone's house than to smell cinnamon. Isn't that like walking into a hug or something?"

The Blueberry Cinnamon Roll Coffee Cake didn't win Sheppard a prize, but competing in the 46th Pillsbury Bake-Off Contest was "one of the best experiences of my life," she says. So when Contest 47 opened, "I just figured, Let's not push it," and she entered only two recipes. This time contestants didn't need votes to qualify as finalists—and Sheppard was again named one of the lucky 100. Her recipe? Lemon-Broccoli Risotto Rounds, made with Green Giant Steamers Cheesy Rice & Broccoli, an eligible product that year. "I thought, Maybe if you took those little Pillsbury Crescent rounds and filled them with the broccoli-rice mixture, it would be similar to *arancini*," Italian rice balls that are one of her brother's favorite dishes. He taste-tested her recipe, and "when he liked it, I knew I could send it in," says Sheppard, who tries a recipe an average of three times before submitting it.

What was it about the coffee cake and the risotto rounds that set them apart from all the other recipes she'd entered over the years? "I think they showcased the ingredients to a better fashion than I had in the past," she says. "I'd been looking at the recipe as a whole, which is fine, but I wasn't looking at showcasing the ingredients." Thinking like a marketer helps, she says: "You want to make your product look the best, and you want to choose recipes that make your product look good."

Her M.O. is challenging but straightforward. "I look at what the eligible ingredients are, and then I try to develop an interesting shape. What could I make out of that that you wouldn't expect?" says Sheppard, who reads *Bon Appétit* and *Cook's Illustrated* magazines and watches *America's Test Kitchen* and *Cook's Country* on

TV. She sees a connection between trying to envision ingredients differently and the teaching she used to do: "I liked having my students look at something in a different way than what they had been used to, so when I cook, it's like an expression of love to me. It's like I'm reaching out to the people closest to me, saying, 'This is how I show you I love you. This is how I'm maybe influencing you or forcing you to try something different to open your mind.'"

Sheppard says she has encouraged others to enter since competing as a finalist. "You'll make friends to last a lifetime," she says. "And it's a challenge. Even if you send in a recipe you're not real sure about, there's that excitement when you're checking your email, that glimmer of hope that keeps all of us going." Her advice for those who have had their recipes rejected: "Don't get discouraged. I'm living proof! Don't take it personally. It's not that they don't like you. Maybe they were looking for something else."

Unless the rules change, Sheppard has only one more opportunity to compete in the Bake-Off Contest, and she plans to increase the number of recipes she submits. Her main goal is to return as a finalist, not necessarily to win the grand prize. "The chances of winning the million dollars are very, very small," she says. "Just being there, the whole experience—there's so much fun there. There's no nasty competition, just all good people."

Sheppard has taken the memory of her grandmother, kneading by her side, along for the Bake-Off ride. "If you talk to your fellow contestants and get to know them, almost always there's been a family member who has influenced their cooking, whether it's Grandma or Mom or Dad," she says. "I think that shows us the link between food and family just can't be broken. It's love, it's history, it's hospitality, it's all good things that make family family."

Mary Hawkes
Prescott, Arizona

CONTEST 35 **Hot and Hearty Heroes**
CONTEST 36 **Mediterranean Sandwich Pockets**
CONTEST 37 **Banana Chocolate Brunch Cake**

As Mary Hawkes was leaving her house to mail a recipe to the 1992 Pillsbury Bake-Off Contest, her husband looked at her and said, "You're not entering *again*, are you?" She had been trying to become a finalist for nearly three decades, since she was 12 years old.

But this time was different. Before she'd even thought of the recipe she was mailing that day, Hawkes had re-evaluated the situation. "I said to myself, You've been entering for so long, and you haven't been chosen. You must be doing something wrong," she says. So she gathered Pillsbury cookbooks, especially those containing Bake-Off recipes, and studied them, trying to get a sense of what the company was looking for. She came to three conclusions: Her previous recipes had too many ingredients, her titles weren't catchy, and her dishes weren't innovative enough. "I was certainly entering recipes that were quite tasty and that my family loved, but to use a cliché, I wasn't thinking outside the box," she says. "When I looked at those things, I realized, OK, let's approach it somewhat differently this year." And so she set about creating recipes with a new perspective.

Sure enough, the Pillsbury team selected one of them, Hot and Hearty Heroes, for that year's competition. What made it innovative? "It was more like an Italian stromboli, and you typically didn't see that in Bake-Off entries" at the time, she says. Then, too, she used Pillsbury's hot roll mix "not as a bread or roll, but to make a sandwich. So I did try to use their product in a somewhat different way."

Hawkes's new approach got her into the next two competitions as well, with her Mediterranean Sandwich Pockets in 1994 and her Banana Chocolate Brunch Cake in 1996. But it was her first competition that really buoyed her confidence. "My attitude changed," she says. "I thought, If my recipe can be chosen as a finalist in this contest, I should enter other contests. And that's when my passion for creating recipes and entering other contests really began."

Hawkes went on to place in or win a slew of cooking competitions—the National Chicken Cooking Contest, the National Beef Cook-Off, the Beringer Great Steak Challenge, and others—racking up prizes that have included a truck, a kitchen remodel, appliances, vacations, and cash. One newspaper called her "the cooking contest queen of Arizona." Hawkes says creating recipes for these contests has been "therapeutic" for her, "the way some people might do painting, some people might do writing, and some people might do jogging or working out."

Although Hawkes has participated in a wide variety of cooking contests, the Pillsbury competition stands out in her memory. "It was just like one big party," she says. "You're there, the 99 other finalists are there, the media is there. You're in this great big room, and everybody is hustling and bustling, people taking photos, people interviewing people, the smell of food. And you're standing there thinking, Wow, I'm part of this."

She laughs as she recalls the time a camera crew set up its equipment right outside her oven door while her Mediterranean Sandwich Pockets were baking. As the photographers conducted an interview in the next mini kitchen, Hawkes's timer went off. "I couldn't get my door open to get my dish out or at least look at it," she says. "I just remember saying, 'You've got to move your camera,' and they were so annoyed with me. I thought, Hey, I've got money on the line here!"

Oven-door traffic notwithstanding, Hawkes's Pillsbury experiences were so positive that she happily recommends the competition to others. In fact, her good friend Connie Stone took her suggestion to enter and became a finalist herself—on her first and only try. Hawkes decided to pack her bags and travel to the Contest, held that year in Orlando, Florida, to cheer on Stone, who competed with a Creamy Lemon-Poppyseed Tart.

Surely Hawkes's advice served her friend well as she entered the Contest. Here, Hawkes shares it with *Smart Cookies*:

- Don't count on getting into the Contest with the recipe handed down from Grandma that the entire family loves. "It may be the absolutely greatest-tasting recipe, but everybody makes it, it's in all the cookbooks, and it's at every potluck around," says Hawkes, who submitted three to seven entries in each Contest. "It's a been-there-done-that kind of recipe. Maybe it isn't creative in and of itself."
- Consider the recipe title a chance to catch the reviewer's attention. "If you can't make the title catchy, make it descriptive without being as long as a dictionary," she says. "The title may well be the first thing they look at."
- Think of how you could use a sponsor ingredient in a new way: "Try to incorporate a creative use of a Pillsbury product."
- Persevere—but stay up-to-date. "Just keep at it, but also try to keep things fresh. Keep up with food trends," says

Hawkes, who reads food magazines online through her local library. "If something was in vogue 10 years ago, that doesn't necessarily mean it's still going to be popular today."

- Read the rules carefully. "Pay attention to the rules because that can mean the difference between having a wonderful recipe submitted and considered and having a wonderful recipe submitted and thrown out," she says.
- Write a clear, complete recipe and then set it aside—twice. "When I create a recipe, I think, OK, it's ready to go, and then I let it sit for a couple of days. Then I look at it again and make sure I didn't forget something. I put it down *again* for another couple of days," Hawkes says. "You need to let it rest and let your brain take a break from it and then go back to it, because maybe, as I've done, you've completely left out an ingredient." She also recommends having someone else proofread the recipe.

As a three-time finalist, Hawkes is no longer eligible to participate in the Pillsbury Bake-Off Contest under current rules, but she continues to enter other cooking competitions. "It's still my passion," she says. Retired from her job as the director of the Better Business Bureau's northern Arizona branch, she will sometimes work on two or three contests simultaneously. Other times she'll go several months without entering any contests if she doesn't find them inspiring. "At this point I really do pick and choose which contests I want to enter," Hawkes says. She's come a long way from the 12-year-old girl who entered the Pillsbury Bake-Off Contest for the first time. "Perseverance," she says, "does eventually pay off!"

Heidi Givler
Lenhartsville, Pennsylvania

CONTEST 46 *Carrot Cupcakes With Coconut Pecan Frosting*

She drag-races for fun. She works full time in IT despite the often-painful effects of lupus. She helps care for relatives who have lupus or dementia. She has successfully organized and run events to raise awareness of her disease, promoting them on local TV news shows. She won a statewide pie-baking contest. And yet for more than 20 years the one thing Heidi Givler couldn't do was get into the Pillsbury Bake-Off Contest.

Not that she wasn't trying hard enough. In the early days Givler would enter upwards of 70 recipes in a single contest, so eager was she to become a finalist. It all started when she was strolling through the Schuylkill County Fair one day, in her home state of Pennsylvania: Noticing the ribbons on pies and other dishes that had won prizes, she felt a tug on her competitive nature, the same tug that had driven her to succeed in science fairs and speech competitions in school. And so she started entering the Bake-Off Contest and persevered—even after a man she was briefly dating told her she'd never become a finalist. Even after the man who would become her husband said the Contest was "fake," with people chosen at random to portray the finalists. Even after, in a crushing turn of events in 2012, her sister died of lupus, at the age of 43.

"I was so upset I didn't want to cook or try anymore," Givler says. "But out of the blue I saw they were having a Pillsbury Bake-Off in 2013." A product on the list of eligible ingredients caught her eye: Green Giant Steamers frozen Honey Dijon Carrots. Givler was no stranger to the use of vegetables in baked goods, having made veggie breads with "pretty much any vegetable," including carrots, she says. She'd even won several county-fair contests in the veggie-bread category. But this time the eligible ingredient wasn't just carrots; it was honey Dijon carrots. What to do with that? "I see all those *Cupcake Wars* shows where they're telling you to add all these crazy ingredients," she says, "and I thought, Well, let's see what the honey Dijon is going to do." So she thawed the carrots, chopped them in a food processor, and added them to a prepared yellow cake mix, along with raisins and pecans. The result was a tasty batter, which she baked as cupcakes. After topping them with cream cheese frosting, a traditional choice for carrot cake, she entered the recipe.

And then she made a crucial decision. "It was at the last minute," she says. "I was sitting there thinking, I like the cupcake part, but why couldn't I try a different frosting?" She re-created the recipe, this time topping the carrot cupcakes with coconut pecan frosting, more commonly used on German chocolate cake. The combination of cupcake and frosting was unexpected, and the pecans in the frosting mirrored the pecans in the cupcakes. She liked the result and entered the new version of the recipe, one of more than 20 she submitted that year.

When General Mills emailed notices to the semifinalists, Givler received one—along with the news that it was her Carrot Cupcakes With Coconut Pecan Frosting that made the list. Home at the time, she quickly texted her husband, Brad, who was mowing the lawn; he's hearing impaired and would have had difficulty understanding her if she'd yelled from a window. "That can't be a real email,"

Brad replied, still convinced that the Contest was fake. Undeterred, Givler started campaigning for online votes, which all 2013 semifinalists needed to become finalists. "I had to parade around town, hanging up signs, calling people, bringing cupcakes everywhere, saying, 'Please vote for me,'" she says. "I was telling every stranger I saw at every mall I was at. People must have thought I was a lunatic." She also campaigned where she works, at a state center for people with disabilities. It was there that she learned she had received enough votes to become a finalist. "I went, 'Yahoo!' really loud, and people came out of their offices.... I'm like, 'I'm going to Vegas, baby!'" she says.

But before Givler could go to Las Vegas, where the 46th Pillsbury Bake-Off Contest was held, she had to prepare—not just to bake her cupcakes but also to manage the effects of lupus, an autoimmune disease that can cause extreme fatigue, pain, photosensitivity, and other symptoms. She arrived two days early to get some rest, and she took extra medication to combat the dizziness she was experiencing and ward off the migraines she sometimes gets. The day of the Contest, she took a warm shower at 4 a.m. because her joints were swollen and achy, and she applied pain-relief patches to her knees and back. She pulled on a compression girdle to help her stand as long as she needed to. And then she dressed and accessorized in purple, the color for lupus awareness: underwear, shirt, socks, sneakers, hair ribbon. She wore two purple bracelets, one for her and one for her sister, and a necklace that contained her sister's thumbprint.

As she marched, teary-eyed, onto the Contest floor, Givler made the "I love you" symbol for the hearing impaired with her hands. Someone else had tears, too: Brad, standing with the onlookers.

"He believes it now," she says. "He said it was the most phenomenal thing."

Today they're both fans of the Pillsbury Bake-Off Contest, and Givler has a new social network of finalists who competed in Las Vegas with her. Several of them, including Victoria Croce (see page 37), even served as judges in one or more of the cooking contests she sponsored at Pennsylvania's Great Allentown Fair to raise awareness of lupus. Givler named the contests, modeled after the TV show *Chopped*, in memory of her sister, Cherylanne Neidlinger.

Now that she's had the Bake-Off experience, Givler is able to advise other home cooks hoping to become finalists. "Try mixing and matching things," she suggests. "Play with your food." For inspiration she likes to watch TV host and chef Alton Brown, especially on his show *Good Eats*, where he explains the science of baking. "He knows his food and his appliances and his tools," Givler says.

Exactly what was it that got her into the Pillsbury Bake-Off Contest after 20-plus years of striking out? She thinks about her recipe and how it fit into the finger-food trend and the get-your-vegetables trend. But of this she is more certain: "Somehow my sister, I believe, got me there," she says. "I feel that she pulled some strings in heaven."

Marie Bruno
Greensboro, Georgia

CONTEST 46 *Decadent Chocolate Hazelnut Tart*

When Marie Bruno started testing her baking skills as a teenager, she had more misses than hits. "But not being one to get discouraged easily," she says, "that only spurred me to do better."

Not being one to get discouraged easily is an understatement. Bruno began entering the Pillsbury Bake-Off Contest in the mid to late 1970s and kept at it, submitting three or four recipes in nearly every competition until she became a finalist in 2013. "Creating a recipe that was worthy of this contest was one of my longtime goals," she says. "And it wasn't the money that motivated me. It was that I had challenged myself and I had to do it." Being notified that she had finally been accepted was "like winning the lottery," she says. "It was a dream come true."

What recipe broke the dry spell? The aptly named Decadent Chocolate Hazelnut Tart, which has a cooked filling of whipping cream, semisweet chocolate, mascarpone cheese, chocolate hazelnut spread, and egg yolks. Spooned into a baked Pillsbury pie crust, the filling is dotted with toasted hazelnuts and decorated with chocolate-hazelnut whipped cream and more hazelnuts. "It's tasty and deceptively easy to make," says Bruno, adding that she was delighted with the "magnificent presentation" of her dish in the Contest 46 recipe magazine.

Bruno had been experimenting with tarts—inspired, she says, by "some of the wonderful tarts featured in the great coffeehouses of Europe"—when the eligible products for Contest 46 were announced. As soon as she saw Jif Chocolate Hazelnut Spread on the list, she knew it would complement the hazelnuts in one of the tarts. "It was a perfect fit for my recipe," she says. "When it came together, it was a magical mouthful!"

One snag: The New Jersey native, who lived in Palm Beach, Florida, for 38 years, has trouble finding hazelnuts anywhere near her current home, on a Georgia cattle ranch. Her solution? She orders them online. Other desserts in which she uses hazelnuts are shortbread and biscotti, including her grandmother's Christmas Molasses Biscotti. "When we were kids, we used to call them jawbreakers," she says. "You really had to dunk them."

Her grandmother, an Italian immigrant, left an indelible impression on Bruno's cooking and baking. "My mom was a good cook, but my Italian grandmother was a great cook," she says. As a child, Bruno thought her grandmother had a "magic pot," because "no matter how many people popped in at dinnertime, there was always enough food to feed them." In a nod to her grandmother's influence, she wants to write an Italian cookbook. "I know there are a million Italian cookbooks, but I've got some different, unique, and easier ways to prepare a lot of traditional Italian foods," she says.

Unless General Mills changes the rules, writing a cookbook would most likely disqualify her from future Pillsbury Bake-Off Contests—but she's not sure she wants to enter again anyway. "It depends on whether something catches my eye, maybe a new ingredient I might try to be creative with. But it takes a lot of energy, and I'm not getting any younger," says Bruno, who has scaled back her work as a real estate broker. Besides all the shopping for ingredients, "it's fine-tuning. You can get the basics down, and just when you think you've got something really good—I'm speaking in my case now—something else will pop into my mind, and I'll say, Oh, wow, I should maybe try that. And then it may work, it may not." Sometimes, too, her taste testers ("I have volunteers everywhere") will tell Bruno they prefer an earlier version of a recipe she's creating. "So we're back to square one," she says.

"There's a lot to developing a recipe that's going to catch the judges' attention, that's going to be food-worthy, tasteful, with a nice presentation," says Bruno, who has had original recipes featured in *Better Homes and Gardens* and one of its cookbooks. "It takes a lot of effort, and I commend every single lady and gentleman who was chosen for the Bake-Off."

Her admiration for her fellow finalists is obvious. "I really, really enjoyed meeting all those wonderful, creative people," she says. "There's an energy, and you get to feed off that energy." Bruno also has high praise for the General Mills employees who staffed the Contest: "I was impressed. To put on an event on that scale, with 100 finalists and 100 stoves, everything worked and all the different ingredients [were properly supplied]—what a huge undertaking."

Bake-Off hopefuls who want to follow Bruno into what she calls "the Super Bowl of baking" may want to adopt her practices:

- ◆ Write down all the ingredients and take notes while you're testing the recipe. "If you do a whole bunch of different recipes, like I do for the Bake-Off Contest, it's really hard if you wait until the last minute," she says. "You will either get confused or forget something."
- ◆ Be fearless with food. "I'm not shy about trying to put some strange or different or odd combinations together and seeing how that would work in a recipe," says Bruno, a big fan of Ina Garten, the host of *Barefoot Contessa*. "You

have to be willing to experiment. Why should you be afraid of food, for goodness' sake?"

- ◆ Keep trying. "Don't give up. If I can [become a finalist], I think anybody can," she says.

"When people ask, 'How do you come up with these recipes?' I say, 'I don't know. I think in food,'" Bruno says. And when they ask for her secret? "I tell everybody the secret ingredient is love. If you don't love what you're doing, you're going to be burning a lot of food or wasting a lot of money on groceries. If you don't love it, don't bother."

CHAPTER 2

Batting a Thousand

GENERAL MILLS SAYS it receives "tens of thousands" of entries for each Pillsbury Bake-Off Contest (the scuttlebutt at the 2014 Contest put the number at 65,000). Only 100 are selected for competition.

Even though the chances of getting into just one Bake-Off Contest are minuscule, Arlene Erlbach has gotten into all three she entered. Marie Valdes and Victoria Croce are two for two. Here, they tell how they beat the odds.

Arlene Erlbach
Morton Grove, Illinois

CONTEST 45 *Smoky Onion-Custard Tarts*
CONTEST 46 *Cranberry Orange Dark Chocolate Flatbread*
CONTEST 47 *Sweet and Salty Chocolate Chip–Maple–Peanut Bars*

You might think that Arlene Erlbach, who was a finalist in all three of the Pillsbury Bake-Off Contests she entered, grew up with a mother who baked the best cake on the block or cooked a mean coq au vin. But you'd be very wrong.

Her mother was so averse to preparing food that when young Arlene received a Junior Bake Set—complete with a mini baking pan and a small box of cake mix—from a friend, she had a hard time getting Mom to take any interest in it. "My mother disliked baking so much that it was months afterward that she'd even used it with me," she says.

But that friend, who lived just four doors away from Erlbach in Shaker Heights, Ohio, came from a home where the oven always seemed to be on, where her mother and grandmother not only enjoyed baking and cooking but also experimented with the new food products of the day. "This was when all the new cake mixes were coming out, after World War II," says Erlbach. "They would buy them a lot and try them, and I really wanted to try them." Erlbach spent a good deal of time at their house, cultivating what would turn out to be a lifelong hobby.

Many years later, another friend told Erlbach about the Pillsbury Bake-Off Contest—specifically, about the 2006 winning recipe, Baked Chicken and Spinach Stuffing, which earned Anna Ginsberg the million-dollar grand prize (see page 135). "I thought I would give [the Contest] a try," Erlbach says. "But I kept putting it off," largely because her work as a teacher, in both special education and English as a second language, was demanding. "And then I just decided I would try it."

She entered a dozen recipes, all appetizers and brunch dishes, in the 2012 Contest, and the Bake-Off team chose the Smoky Onion-Custard Tarts from her brunch entries. "This is my take on things, but I think it's easier to get in with a brunch dish," she says. In the next Contest, of her 20 entries, another brunch recipe—Cranberry Orange Dark Chocolate Flatbread—was selected.

For her third and final Contest, in 2014, Erlbach went all out and submitted 40 recipes, covering every category. This time Pillsbury passed up her brunch dishes and chose a dessert, Sweet and Salty Chocolate Chip–Maple–Peanut Bars. Although Erlbach was thrilled to be returning to the Bake-Off Contest, she was surprised the bars made the cut. She had figured that her "absolutely best recipe"—cinnamon rolls baked with a filling of cream cheese, bacon, and maple extract and topped with maple frosting and pecans—would be chosen, but she has a theory about why it wasn't. In 2014, Bake-Off recipes were accepted in two rounds: Desserts and sides were due first, and breakfasts and dinners seven weeks later. "I think that if you got in one round and if you have something spectacular for the second round, they're not going to choose it," she says. "That's just my opinion, but that's what I think."

Erlbach has other theories as well. For one thing, she believes it's difficult to get in with a dish that contains low-fat or sugar-free ingredients. She recalls the time she submitted a recipe for a chicken braid that called for low-fat cream cheese and sugar-free jam. "Somebody else sent in almost the same thing but with no low-fat ingredients, and theirs got in," she says. "I couldn't believe it. It was just like mine, but they used regular ingredients! And for sure even if your low-fat thing gets in, it's not going to win."

Another theory occurred to Erlbach after she studied the top four winning recipes in the 2014 Contest (Peanutty Pie Crust Clusters, Creamy Corn–Filled Sweet Peppers, Cuban-Style Sandwich Pockets, and Chocolate Doughnut Poppers). "[The judges] seem to like little cute things. It probably goes with the small-bite trend," she says. Erlbach also observed that the four recipes used few appliances—no food processors and only one hand mixer among them.

Beyond her theories and observations, Erlbach has this advice for home cooks who want to become Bake-Off finalists:

- "Think outside the box, but not too outside it," she says—that is, not too high-end or gourmet.
- Read food magazines for ideas. "I think *Taste of Home* is perfect for people who want to enter Pillsbury," she says. "And I think with *Food Network* and *Rachael Ray* [*Every Day*], you get an idea of trends that everybody might be interested in and also trends that are over the top."
- Don't enter a recipe that yields more than two dozen if you're using muffin tins. Most people don't have enough muffin tins to accommodate more than 24, she says.
- Avoid equipment that's out of the ordinary, even popover pans.
- Keep in mind that General Mills will look for a certain number of recipes to qualify for the smaller prizes in a given Contest—for example, peanut butter recipes that will be contenders for the Jif Peanut Butter Award, if there is one.

- Don't submit a recipe that contains a low-fat or sugar-free ingredient unless there's a category for it.
- Limit your ingredients to what most people can find in their neighborhood grocery stores. Erlbach learned this lesson after developing a recipe that called for a package of smoked trout; a friend pointed out that a small-town supermarket was unlikely to carry it. "I think if you live in New York City or Chicago, you have to realize that not every place is like that in terms of ingredients, ease of getting them, or things people are knowledgeable about," she says.
- "Really follow the directions!" she says.

If Erlbach's tips seem particularly thorough, that may be because she has experience in the advice business: Some of the 40-plus books she has written provide guidance on the challenges children face in school, at home, and beyond. In *The Kids' Business Book*, she explains to preteens how they can undertake a project and make it a success—a topic she is well familiar with.

Now retired from both the Bake-Off Contest and her teaching job, Erlbach has been entering competitions sponsored by *Taste of Home*. She won the magazine's Easy Holiday Baking contest with her simplified Sacher torte recipe, and its Merriest Potluck contest with her Black-Bottomed Brandy Bites. *Taste of Home* has featured other recipes of hers as well, including her Pancetta Pear and Pecan Puffs.

Although current Pillsbury rules prohibit three-time finalists from competing in the Bake-Off Contest again, this may not be the end of Erlbach's Doughboy days. Her husband, Herb, who is one of her taste testers, is considering entering in the future. Having accompanied his wife to the competitions, he has his own theory:

that finalists improve their chances of returning by being gracious and reliable. Which could at least partly explain Erlbach's repeated success.

She'd be delighted to see Herb win his own spot in the Contest. "The Pillsbury Bake-Off was just amazing," she says. "The way you're treated, all the nice people you meet—just everything about it."

Marie Valdes
Brandon, Florida

CONTEST 46 *Honey Chicken and Corn Rafts*
CONTEST 47 *Spinach Dip–Stuffed Garlic Rolls*

The first time Marie Valdes did her grocery shopping after she and her husband moved from Queens, New York, to Brandon, Florida, in 1987, she went to the deli counter and asked for Pecorino Romano cheese. "The deli man just looked at me," she says. "So I said, 'I need a pound of grated Locatelli cheese,'" thinking he might recognize the brand name. Still the man didn't know what she wanted. He called the manager over, and Valdes explained, "It's the cheese you put on spaghetti." The supermarket, it turned out, had no fresh Italian grating cheese at all. "I came home and said to my husband, 'We have to move!'"

Food has long played an important role in Valdes's life, from the time she grew up in a predominantly Italian and Greek neighborhood of Queens to the present, which finds her in an enviable perch: She's a two-time Pillsbury Bake-Off finalist who got in both times she entered. Her success is perhaps unsurprising when you consider that she started buying Bake-Off recipe magazines as a teenager. What *is* surprising is that it took her from her teens to her 50s to submit a recipe. "My mother kept saying, 'Why don't you enter the Contest?'" Valdes says. "But I felt very intimidated. It was such a big contest, with such a big prize, that I didn't think I would do well." Still, she promised her mother that one day she would enter.

Valdes lost her mother in 2013. A month later, the first deadline for entries in the 46th Pillsbury Bake-Off Contest was approaching, and her husband reminded her of her promise. So she read the rules "very, very carefully," she says. Around the same time, she happened to watch a TV show about then first lady Michelle Obama's White House garden, with its honeybees and vegetables. The program stimulated her creative juices, and in short order Valdes developed a recipe called Honey Chicken and Corn Rafts, made with Pillsbury refrigerated pizza dough. "The inspiration was the honey from the honeybees and how Mrs. Obama also grew vegetables," she says. "I made it a couple of times, tweaking the ingredients and trying to do it in different shapes until I was happy with the end result."

That was the only recipe she submitted in 2013. It went on to semifinalist status, and when it received enough votes, Valdes won her first finalist spot at the Pillsbury Bake-Off Contest. She didn't take home a prize, but her mind-set changed nonetheless. "After you win Pillsbury once, your life revolves around Pillsbury dough and all the different things you can do with it," she says. "I think one of the most difficult things for people is, What recipe hasn't been done? But I think there's always something else out there."

Her second finalist recipe proves her point. At a family get-together to watch football on TV, "everybody was dipping their garlic rolls into the spinach dip," she says. "I said, 'What if I put the spinach dip *in* the garlic rolls?'" And so her Spinach Dip–Stuffed Garlic Rolls were born. She did have to rework the recipe a couple of times to make sure the filling wasn't too wet, but of her four entries in 2014, it was by far her favorite. With the three others, "I was just trying too hard," she says. In fact, when she was notified by email that she was a finalist, she was afraid to see which recipe had been chosen. "I would not have been happy if it wasn't that one," she says. "I was happy that Pillsbury picked the right one."

She considers herself lucky that her favorite recipe was chosen and says she learned a lesson: "If I'm not 100 percent positive and happy and content and I feel it's a great recipe, I won't submit it.... I don't want second best; I want what I feel would be the best I could do with an idea." Valdes's Spinach Dip–Stuffed Garlic Rolls not only returned her to the Bake-Off Contest but also won Pillsbury's Clever Twist Award, earning her $5,000 and bragging rights as a creative cook (see recipe, page 154).

After her consecutive successes as a finalist, the *Tampa Tribune* asked Valdes what her secret was. "I said, 'I don't think there is a secret,'" she says. But she does underscore the importance of following the rules and offers this advice:

- Research your recipe to be sure it's original. "You may have a fantastic idea," she says, "but you have to make sure it hasn't been done before by somebody else who had that fantastic idea, too."
- Consider the tastes of the general population. One reason Valdes believes her Spinach Dip–Stuffed Garlic Rolls were chosen is that they appealed to a variety of people, including children. Another reason: She combined two popular dishes.
- Keep the recipe simple. "Some people want to get too exotic with the recipes, and I don't think that's Pillsbury's forte," she says. "I consider them the all-American baking company."

A self-described perfectionist and consummate researcher who owns more than 500 cookbooks, Valdes says the best thing about becoming a finalist was "the recognition that I did something good, that I created a recipe that Pillsbury felt was worthy of the Contest." The next-best thing? "It has motivated me even more to go outside the Pillsbury arena and enter other contests," she says. "I love seeing all the other people's creativity. We also feed off each other and encourage each other. I love when I see a recipe and think, That was brilliant—how did you come up with that idea?" In 2015 she won the Sebastiani Vineyards and Winery "Pizza My Way" contest.

Meanwhile, Valdes continues to think of potential recipes for the Pillsbury Bake-Off Contest. "It keeps you creative," she says. But one thing has changed since she last competed: She no longer works at a facility with 1,200 employees, a large pool of eligible taste tasters who gave her feedback on the dishes she brought in. Today she works at home, as a benefits specialist for a large pharmacy. "It's nobody but me and my husband," she says, so she has been sending her baked goods to his office.

Her main motivation for entering the Contest has always been the million-dollar grand prize, but that's "followed very closely by the people you meet and the amazing time you have just being a finalist," she says. "It is by far the best thing that has ever happened in my life. You did something that was recognized, and you were rewarded for it. I think it's the only contest you go to that even if you lose, you come away a winner."

BATTING A THOUSAND

Victoria Croce
Palmyra, Pennsylvania

CONTEST 46 *Chorizo Party Appetizers*
CONTEST 47 *New Orleans Andouille Shrimp Pizza*

Victoria Croce had never entered a cooking contest before when she asked her sisters to taste-test her Chorizo Party Pucks for the 46th Pillsbury Bake-Off Contest in 2013. She prepared the recipe two ways: with plantains and with mango. Her sisters preferred the plantains, but Croce decided to go with the mango. Not only did it moisten the chorizo filling, she says, but "it gave a much better color presentation for pictures."

Having read the Contest rules and instructions, Croce knew that appearance was important (it was one of four criteria that year, along with taste, creativity, and consumer appeal). So even though she was a cooking-contest novice, she trusted her judgment, and her decision panned out: The Bake-Off team selected her colorful chorizo-mango starters, one of 13 recipes she'd submitted, as a semifinalist entry, renaming it Chorizo Party Appetizers. After it received enough online votes—appearance played an even bigger role here, given that photos accompanied all the semifinalist recipes—Croce was a finalist in the first Pillsbury Bake-Off Contest she had ever entered.

She may have been a newcomer to contests, but Croce was an experienced home cook, influenced by her father, who owned an Italian restaurant and taught her mother how to cook, and her grandfather. Both were innovative in the kitchen, and their creativity rubbed off on Croce, who considers herself more of a cook than a baker. "I baked as a child, beginning at eight years old," when she received an Easy-Bake Oven, she says. "Cooking came a little later, and cooking is what became my passion."

When the 47th Pillsbury Bake-Off Contest opened and Croce was trying to create an original pizza recipe to enter, she followed her father's example and bypassed the traditional choice of cheese, mozzarella. "He always used provolone" on pizza at his restaurant, she says. "So I remembered that, and I thought, That's what I'm going to do." She also tried to come up with uncommon pizza toppings. "I really like eggplant, and I don't see it that much," she remembers thinking. To the eggplant she added smoked spicy sausage, shrimp, and red bell pepper, and the resulting recipe—New Orleans Andouille Shrimp Pizza, one of two she entered that year—got Croce into the Pillsbury Bake-Off Contest the second time in a row.

Most of Croce's recipes occur to her when she's not trying to think of an idea. "It's weird," she says. "I'll be lying down, trying to sleep, and an idea for a recipe will pop into my head. I'll quickly get up and jot it down." She finds recipe creation relaxing and thinks of new Bake-Off ideas between Contests, even before the eligible products are announced. "I have a folder full of ideas," she says, explaining that she sometimes writes down ingredients or the method of a recipe as a guide for herself. Then, once the rules and sponsor products are announced, "I just tweak it."

What advice does she have for home cooks who want to emulate her success? "I would say just throw some ideas and some ingredients around in your head and try to mentally picture with your taste buds what that would taste like, just to give you an idea of will it work or won't it," says Croce, who participated in the

Bake-Off Contest under her former name, Victoria Potts. "You can almost taste it in your mind. Then try it."

With two finalist experiences under her belt, Croce has one more chance to attend the Bake-Off Contest unless the rule changes. She notes that some three-time finalists have said they'd like General Mills to drop the rule so that they can participate as often as they wish. "I'm kind of on the fence about that," she says. "I feel that three times is good. Let other people have a chance to feel that experience. I'm good with that."

Croce has no plans to alter her recipe strategy to improve her remaining shot at the grand prize. Since finding out about the Bake-Off Contest while surfing the internet in 2013, she's been mostly motivated by the creative challenge, though "the prize was certainly attractive, too," she says. "I'm just not really competitive. I enjoy winning like the next guy, but I'm more a giving than receiving type of person." Her attitude extends to sharing recipes (Bake-Off recipes must be original and unpublished when General Mills receives them, which pretty much rules out disseminating them before they've been judged). "When I come up with a recipe that's good, I always share it," says Croce, who enjoys watching *The Chew* on TV. "I'm not one of those people who come up with a recipe and won't share it. I think it's ridiculous that some people take their recipes to the grave. I just don't see the point."

Being in the Bake-Off Contest definitely increased her confidence, Croce says. It has even touched the lives of everyone she has told about it: "It's a good story when you're talking to people and they're talking about food and you mention that you were in the Bake-Off. Then they want to hear your story. They enjoy it; they're impressed. They say, 'Oh, I never knew anybody who was in the

Bake-Off.'" What did she like most about the Contest? Croce can't single anything out. "Everything was just perfect, the full package," she says. "It was like being Cinderella for a weekend."

See also Christina Verrelli (page 131), who became a finalist both times she entered and won the grand prize the second time.

CHAPTER 3

Resilience, Their Secret Ingredient

FACED WITH ADVERSITY—depression, cancer, a series of strokes, the loss of a loved one—these home cooks bounced back, displaying a strength that took them all the way to the Pillsbury Bake-Off Contest floor. Here's how resilience made finalists out of Shana Butler, Michele Kusma, Carole Resnick, Brenda Watts, and Linda Drumm.

Shana Butler
San Diego

CONTEST 45 *Peachy Cream Cheese Appetizers*
CONTEST 47 *Chicken Florentine "Gnocchi"*

After Shana Butler tore her rotator cuff while on the job as a drafting services aide in 2011, she was out on disability and trying to cope with the pain. Her boss met her for lunch every week or two and at one point told Butler she was starting to show signs of depression. Later in that conversation, Butler happened to mention that she had received an email announcing that the Pillsbury Bake-Off Contest was accepting recipes for the 2012 competition, the 45th. As she recalls, her boss told her, "Why don't you enter it? It will give you something else to focus on and get your mind off everything you're going through and your pain."

"So I thought about it and came home that day and just started bouncing around some different ideas," says Butler, who has been cooking and baking since childhood but had never created a recipe before. Within a week she had a couple of dishes to test on family and friends, who came over and gave her creations the thumbs-up. But before they left, Butler went to the kitchen to find a use for her leftover ingredients: peach preserves, cream cheese, Pillsbury Crescent dough sheets, a lime, shallots, and fresh cilantro, to which she added cumin and chili powder. "I wanted to get everything out of my house while I had people there to eat it," Butler says. "I just threw something together." That something was such a hit with her taste testers that they insisted she enter it in the Bake-Off Contest. "I can't even tell you how shocked I was," says Butler, who had to figure out how to re-create the recipe, since she hadn't measured the ingredients.

She was shocked once again when the Bake-Off team called her to say that she was a finalist—and that of the three recipes she'd entered, they'd picked her creation of leftover ingredients, Peachy Cream Cheese Appetizers. "I just started screaming and laughing," she says. "It made me forget about every ounce of pain I had. It was one of the highlights of my life. I was just so happy." And things only went up from there: Butler was featured in *The San Diego Union-Tribune*, and she prepared her recipe on *San Diego Living*, a local TV show. "I really felt like a rock star," she says.

Butler humbly refers to the appetizers as her "throwaway recipe," but the truth is, there was a good bit of knowledge behind it. "At the time, I was really into the Food Network, and Bobby Flay was the It man for me," she says, referring to the celebrity chef who is known for using heat in his Southwestern dishes. "So I was watching a lot of his shows, and I just remembered that the cumin and the chili powder and the lime juice go well with sweet or savory." She was also influenced by the food culture in San Diego, with its taco shops, Mexican restaurants, and abundant produce. "We have grocery stores here that cater to the Hispanic population, so you can go in there and find cactus and probably 10, 15 types of chile peppers," says Butler, who was born in Kansas City, Kansas. "I love Mexican food and the types of produce we have available to us that aren't available in different parts of the U.S."

But Mexican food is only one of her favorite cuisines; her love of Italian food drove the recipe that got her into her next Bake-Off Contest, the 47th. (She submitted seven recipes in the intervening competition, but none made it in.) This time her creativity took her down an entirely different path. Whereas she believes her peachy–cream cheese recipe made the cut because of its unusual combination of sweet and savory flavors, her finalist recipe in Contest 47 had a more traditional flavor profile. And yet it was exceedingly innovative.

At the outset of the 47th competition, Butler knew she wanted to try creating pasta from Pillsbury refrigerated dough. That may sound like a long shot, but she was banking on an earlier experience, when she had successfully boiled Pillsbury refrigerated crusty French loaf to make pretzels. "I knew if I boiled that dough, it would cook all the way through," she says. But where to go from there? An idea started brewing in her mind subliminally, as a commercial played over and over on TV. "I don't know if it was Bird's Eye or what, but they kept advertising chicken Florentine, chicken Florentine, chicken Florentine," she says. "It was driving me nuts." During the same time, several of the food programs she was watching on TV featured recipes for gnocchi, Italian pasta dumplings often made with potatoes. Even though she put gnocchi on a mental list of dishes she wanted to try someday, it didn't click with her as a Bake-Off recipe.

Then one day she was walking through the supermarket in search of Pillsbury ideas. "I was just looking from side to side, and I was like, 'What can I make? What can I make?'" she says. When she saw gnocchi on the shelf, she thought of the boiled dough and figured the texture might be similar. Her first step, she decided, would have to be cooking and eating gnocchi for the first time. So she bought a package of gnocchi and a tube of Pillsbury refrigerated crusty French loaf dough, then prepared both—chicken Florentine style—and asked two friends and her nephew to taste-test them. "They couldn't tell the difference" between the real gnocchi and the Pillsbury version, she says. "They wouldn't stop eating it. They just loved it." At that point Butler knew she had an entry for the Bake-Off Contest, and it wound up being one of the 14 or so recipes she submitted. "Everything about that recipe"—both the gnocchi and the chicken Florentine—"was new to me," she says, proving that you don't have to stick with what you know to become a finalist in the Bake-Off Contest.

Neither of Butler's finalist recipes earned her a prize, but she felt like a winner anyway, especially because of "the amazing people that I met, from my fellow competitors all the way up to the people who worked for Pillsbury. I have some lifelong friends that I came away with." She encourages others to enter—"It's an awesome experience that's unlike anything else"—and has been trying to persuade her father to submit recipes. He developed a few for Contest 47 but declined to enter them. "He wasn't real confident with what he had created, but he's been thinking about it ever since the last Bake-Off," Butler says.

Will she enter again herself? "Heck yes!" she says with a laugh. In fact, she has two recipes ready to go, provided that they meet the criteria of a future Contest; one is an entry she held back from the 2014 competition. "Not to be cocky, but I'm really confident that one of these two recipes is going to get me into the next Bake-Off," she says. "They're just as far outside the box as making pasta with bread dough." Her advice for others: "Listen to the feedback you get from your friends and family. If I had not listened to that feedback, I never would have entered the recipe that got me into the Bake-Off. And I would not be where I am today."

Where she is today is a good place—unafraid to test ideas, capable of preparing a meal without a recipe, and stimulated by her new hobby, which she shares with new friends. Her boss's suggestion in 2011 that she enter the Bake-Off Contest was on target. "I enjoy thinking of new recipes, period, not just for the Bake-Off," she says. "I get a kick out of it." Will she continue developing recipes if she becomes a finalist for the third and last time? Butler already has that scenario planned: "I enjoy it so much that after I use up my third try at the Bake-Off, one of the first things I want to do is write a cookbook."

RESILIENCE, THEIR SECRET INGREDIENT

Michele Kusma
Columbus, Ohio

CONTEST 46 *Blueberry Sour Cream Pancakes*
CONTEST 47 *Chewy Gingersnaps With White Chocolate Drizzle*

Michele Kusma used to be so casual about entering the Pillsbury Bake-Off Contest that she doesn't even recall when she started submitting recipes. If she happened to see the Contest advertised on a product while she was in the supermarket, she would say to herself, Maybe I'll go home and think about a recipe. "Sometimes I would remember, sometimes I would forget," she says. "It was just an offhand thing to me." When she did remember, she submitted just one recipe, which was never selected for competition.

That all changed in 2013, when she had fully recovered from a recurrence of breast cancer. Her first diagnosis came when she was 28 years old, and the recurrence 18 years later, in 2011. "The second time, the treatments really threw me for a loop," she says, explaining that she was too sick to cook or bake, much as she loved to. "I was just worn down and worn out from everything. And so as I started to recover, one of the joys that I had was actually starting to prepare food and do things for my family again." In early 2013 she entered the Man-o-Manischewitz Cook-Off, another contest she had only casually considered in the past, and for the first time she became a finalist, with her Sweet & Spicy Seared Tuna. Kusma says she enjoyed competing at the Manischewitz cook-off so much that she decided to change her approach to the Pillsbury Bake-Off Contest, which had started accepting entries again. She remembers thinking, "This time I'm going to put more effort into

Pillsbury, and I'm not just going to submit one. I'm going to really research it and see what recipes they're looking for and get a better handle on exactly what I'm doing."

Kusma entered 10 recipes in the 2013 Bake-Off Contest, all of them more innovative than her previous submissions. "They were simple yet creative, and they used the Pillsbury product in a different way. And I got a hit!" she says. General Mills chose her Blueberry Sour Cream Pancakes, made from Pillsbury refrigerated sugar cookie dough, as a semifinalist recipe, and once it received enough online votes, Kusma was a bona fide Bake-Off finalist.

How did she come up with her idea for turning cookie dough into pancakes? "I was standing in front of all the Pillsbury products in the grocery store, and I was thinking about breakfasts and looking at their products," she says. Reading the label on a tube of sugar cookie dough, she had a lightbulb moment. "A lot of these ingredients really kind of match up with what you might make into a waffle or pancake batter," she recalls thinking. "Well, it's going to be very sweet if I do a pancake batter with this. What could I add that might tone down the sugar and loosen it up? Ooh, sour cream would add a little bit of acidity, and that might balance it out more. And of course eggs, to help it rise a little bit more and loosen up the batter."

Shortly after being named a finalist in both the Manischewitz and Pillsbury contests, Kusma was profiled in *The Columbus* (Ohio) *Dispatch*. In an inspiring interview, she told the newspaper, "When you survive cancer, you live every day to the fullest and you try to accomplish as much as you can." Staying true to those words, she entered the next Pillsbury Bake-Off Contest with 34 recipes, and once again she became a finalist, this time with her gluten-free Chewy Gingersnaps With White Chocolate Drizzle.

Not that she loves gingersnaps or follows a gluten-free diet; Kusma doesn't limit her contest recipes to her personal tastes. A former teacher of gifted middle-school students, she says, "I have always prided myself on my creativity and adapting of things to meet the needs of all my different students, so I feel like I can translate that into recipe creation as well. I try to not just take into account my likes." When the gingersnap idea came to her, she says, "I wasn't afraid to create it and adapt things for other people...and step outside my comfort zone."

Why did her gingersnaps and pancakes make it into the Bake-Off Contest over her other entries? "I think the goal of Pillsbury in this contest is to find recipes that will appeal to their consumers, and gingersnaps are a good Christmas cookie," says Kusma, whose two Bake-Off Contests took place in November. "The pancakes, I think, were just something original and did something different with sugar cookie dough. Again, I go back to the consumer appeal: I think their sugar cookie dough is probably very popular."

A self-described perfectionist, she says, "I will practice things over and over until I get them right." But her advice for Bake-Off hopefuls doesn't include striving for perfection. "To me it seems that the key is a simple, easy-to-follow recipe that uses their products in a unique way," says Kusma, a self-taught cook and baker who watches recipe tutorials on YouTube. "I think the best thing to do is to basically be creative and simple in what you're trying to do. It shouldn't have a million steps."

With only one more finalist turn left unless General Mills changes the rules, Kusma says she keeps a computer file of Bake-Off ideas, the best of which have occurred to her in the shower. They're just thoughts, not fully formed recipes, with one exception:

a dish she envisioned while driving home one night after competing in her first Bake-Off Contest. "I remember this so vividly," she says of the recipe, which calls for Pillsbury frosting, an eligible ingredient in the Contest in which she had just participated. She recalls thinking, "I've got to test this. I think I have everything I need in the house. I'm going to get home and test it out right now." And so she did, to great success. But when the eligible products for the next Contest were announced, frosting wasn't on the list. "That idea is still tucked away in case frosting turns out to be an ingredient," she says.

Looking back on her two Bake-Off Contests, Kusma laughs as she describes meeting the Pillsbury Doughboy, a human outfitted in an enormous costume. "That was awesome, being able to press his belly and he actually giggled," she says. "But the whole experience is just amazing—being flown to a different city and being treated so nicely and meeting other cooking friends."

Kusma seems to be living up to her 2013 newspaper quote about trying to accomplish as much as she can: Between then and late 2016, she racked up no fewer than 15 cooking-competition honors, from companies such as Dole, Eggland's Best, and Farm Rich as well as the World Food Championships. Being in the Bake-Off Contest, she says, "does give you the confidence that you can do it and it is possible."

RESILIENCE, THEIR SECRET INGREDIENT

Carole Resnick
Cleveland

CONTEST 42 *Mexican Egg Salad Wraps*

In life, as in the kitchen, things don't always go as planned. Few people know that better than Carole Resnick, whose career as a psychology professor was thwarted by a series of strokes she suffered shortly after completing her Ph.D., at the age of 46. Unable to teach college, she was profoundly disappointed. But she was also able to give more attention to her hobby, taking it to a level that has brought her both excitement and the meaningful satisfaction that comes from helping others.

A home cook and baker, Resnick started entering recipe contests. Along the way, she learned something about herself: "I love thinking of new recipes," she says. Her first major cooking-contest honor came in 2003, when she was recognized for her potato side dish in the Sutter Home Build a Better Burger competition. Three years later, the Pillsbury Bake-Off Contest chose her Southwestern Egg Salad Wraps, changed the title to Mexican Egg Salad Wraps, and called Resnick with the news that she was a finalist. "I was very, very excited," she says. "I almost didn't believe it." But of the 40 recipes she'd entered that year, the wraps were her least favorite. In fact, she had created the dish to feed the children next door, whom she'd been tutoring, and had pulled together ingredients that she happened to have on hand: eggs, guacamole, limes, green chiles, fresh cilantro, onion, tortillas. "You know—necessity is the mother of invention," she says.

She may not have loved the recipe she was competing with, but she thoroughly enjoyed the Bake-Off Contest. "It was a great experience. I'm disabled, and they were so accommodating," says Resnick, who used a cane at the competition but today has a walker. One General Mills employee carried her ingredients from the refrigerator to her mini kitchen, and another took her prepared entry to the judges. The hotel staff was also eager to help. "The bed was so high that I couldn't get onto it, and they sent up a step stool for me," she says. Resnick wants other people with disabilities to know that they shouldn't hesitate to enter the Bake-Off Contest. "If you have any kind of disability, they will accommodate it," she says. "You shouldn't let that discourage you from entering the Pillsbury Bake-Off."

Resnick has continued to enter the competition, cutting back to about five recipes in the more recent ones, but hasn't made it back as a finalist. She has, however, won so many smaller contests and sweepstakes that she has single-handedly donated about 30 KitchenAid stand mixers—her prizes—to nonprofit organizations. And she sent a "really good blender" to the Gathering Place, an Ohio nonprofit that helps cancer patients, survivors, and their families with support and classes. Resnick herself is a two-time breast cancer survivor.

As if donating useful appliances to worthwhile organizations weren't altruistic enough, Resnick voluntarily helps other people learn how to win prizes as well. Anyone can visit her blog, Cybercook's Cooking Corner (cybercookscookingcorner.blogspot.com), where she frequently updates a list of contests, sweepstakes, and links to entry forms. "I like to see people win," she says. "That makes me very happy." It especially makes her happy to know that someone has won a prize after reading about the contest on her blog.

So eager is Resnick to provide helpful information to others that she volunteers the names of the cooking and baking blogs she

RESILIENCE, THEIR SECRET INGREDIENT

recommends: Melissa's Southern Style Kitchen (melissassouthernstylekitchen.com), Will Cook for Smiles (willcookforsmiles.com), Noble Pig (noblepig.com), Ask Chef Dennis: A Culinary Journey (askchefdennis.com), and Off the Hook on the Plate (offthehookontheplate.com).

In the same spirit, she offers this advice to anyone who wants to become a finalist in the Pillsbury Bake-Off Contest—or any contest:

- Make an appetizer version of your entrée, or vice versa. Then your recipe will have a chance in two categories, not just one. "This, of course, involves increasing or decreasing portion size as well as adjusting cooking or baking time," she says.
- Change the main ingredient in your recipe—for instance, replace beef with chicken. That way, you can enter two recipes with one idea. "Here you would have to change herbs or spices," Resnick says. "What goes with one does not always go with the other. You may have to adjust cooking time; it takes longer to cook beef than chicken."
- Make three significant changes to an existing recipe, and the new recipe will most likely be considered original.
- "Try anything," she says. "Even if the recipe sounds weird, the judges may like it. Just enter. The worst they can do is not choose it."

Why did her own recipe make it into the Bake-Off Contest? "Pillsbury likes easy," she surmises. "I almost have to work backwards on Pillsbury, because I'm a from-scratch cook and baker." Her method is to make a recipe once, taste the results, and adjust the ingredients accordingly; rarely does she feel the need to prepare the dish again. "I've been doing this a long, long time," she says. "I've been baking since I was 10 years old."

Resnick isn't certain she'll enter another Bake-Off Contest. Her decision depends on two things: the location (she's no longer willing to fly, given that air travel has become more onerous) and whether it requires voting. "I will not enter a voting contest, and I will not vote in a voting contest," she says. "They're popularity contests, and they have nothing to do with your recipe." Even if she doesn't enter, she'll continue dreaming up recipes, which she finds both stimulating and relaxing. Ready to jot down ideas at all hours, she keeps a notepad next to her bed at night. "I'm always thinking of recipes," she says.

RESILIENCE, THEIR SECRET INGREDIENT

Brenda Watts
Gaffney, South Carolina

CONTEST 45 *Caramelized Peach Upside-Down Coffee Cake*
CONTEST 46 *Chocolate Cherry Soufflé Cupcakes*
CONTEST 47 *Macaroon–Peanut Butter–Chocolate Tartlets*

Brenda Watts remembers her grandmother Helen Mae McNamara as a wise woman, an inspiring worker (she was a Rosie the Riveter in World War II), and an excellent cook who was known throughout Ypsilanti, Michigan, for her creative dishes. Watts fondly recalls the times McNamara gave her a big hug, then showed her the Pillsbury Bake-Off Contest's latest recipe magazine and said, "Someday, sweetie, your grandma is going to be a finalist, and you're going to see my recipe in this cookbook." Sadly, McNamara died in 1982 without achieving her goal.

Sixteen years later, Watts was a stay-at-home mother of three when she received devastating news: Doctors said she had a brain tumor and gave her three weeks to three months to live. "They said there was nothing they could do," she says. "Fortunately, things took a turn, and I survived." The experience prompted some soul-searching. "I realized how precious our lives are," says Watts. "And I don't know why, but I got to thinking of my grandma and how her dream had never come true. I thought, Gee, if I could just fulfill her dream, it would be like a double blessing, because I had always wanted to do something like that, too."

Initially, the idea of entering the Pillsbury Bake-Off Contest intimidated Watts; after all, it had turned down decades' worth of recipes from her grandmother, whom she considered a superior cook and baker. Watts's daughter tried to persuade her to enter a local contest in Gaffney, South Carolina, where they lived, and once Watts had spent time educating herself in the practice of recipe writing, she agreed. Both mother and daughter won the contest. "That kind of encouraged me: Well, maybe you ain't so bad!" Watts says.

With the boost in confidence, Watts started entering the Pillsbury Bake-Off Contest in 2000, creating recipes, testing them on her husband, and submitting 10 to 20 each time. But the years passed without a bite. She won smaller contests sponsored by Betty Crocker but heard nothing from Pillsbury. As she writes on her blog, BakingBrenda (bakingbrenda.blogspot.com), "There were times I thought maybe that dream wasn't meant to be, but then I could swear I felt my grandma up above, saying to me, 'Come on, sweetie, you can do this. Keep trying.' So I would reach within myself and say, 'Come on, Brenda, you have just got to fulfill your grandma's dream.'"

After entering a few recipes in 2011, she left for Tennessee to be with her daughter, whose husband had just been deployed overseas. "At the last minute, I had this recipe in my head," Watts says. Away from home and with no time to buy the ingredients and try her idea, she decided she would take a chance and enter a recipe without testing it. So she listed all the ingredients, estimated their amounts, and wrote out the method she envisioned. "That's not going to make it in," she remembers thinking as she submitted the recipe.

She was wrong. Pillsbury chose her untested dish, Caramelized Peach Upside-Down Coffee Cake, for competition, making Watts a finalist in the Bake-Off Contest for the first time. She had fulfilled her grandmother's dream.

RESILIENCE, THEIR SECRET INGREDIENT

Surely McNamara would have been impressed with her granddaughter's creativity as well as her ability to accurately estimate the baking time, amounts, and interaction of ingredients in a dish she'd never made. The recipe calls for turning Pillsbury refrigerated sugar cookie dough into cake batter by combining it with baking powder, eggs, and half-and-half, which is poured over a mixture of sliced peaches, butter, brown sugar, and cinnamon. After the coffee cake is baked, it's inverted, topped with a warm glaze of peach preserves and orange juice, and then sprinkled with chopped pecans.

The peach coffee cake was a breakfast recipe; the next time the Bake-Off Contest opened, Watts had her sights set on the dessert category, armed with her experience of turning sugar cookie dough into cake batter. "The cookie dough has this beautiful texture, and you can create a lot with it," says Watts, who enjoys reading *Bon Appétit* magazine. "I thought, Well, how about I make something that tries to melt in your mouth? What if I could combine a soufflé and a cake together and get that texture to be just like a dream, a big puffy cloud?" So she folded beaten egg whites into a mixture of cookie dough, egg yolks, half-and-half, and chocolate hazelnut spread to make an airy batter, which she baked in cupcake liners. Then, because "cherry goes so well with chocolate," she filled each cupcake with cherry preserves and topped it with chocolate frosting and a maraschino cherry. Pillsbury not only chose Watts's Chocolate Cherry Soufflé Cupcakes for competition but also put them on the cover of the Contest 46 recipe magazine.

Watts was delighted to compete again, but her second turn didn't go as smoothly as her first. She had decided to pipe the frosting on the cupcakes but was given a pastry bag with the wrong size coupler. And one of the two pairs of beaters she needed contained two left-sided attachments, so a Bake-Off Contest employee had to run one attachment back and forth to the hotel kitchen to be washed and dried (the finalists' workstations don't have running water). "That's what I love about Pillsbury. They go above and beyond helping you if you have a problem arise in the competition," she says. Still, waiting for clean beaters—and they had to be spotless, given that Watts was beating egg whites—slowed her down, and she submitted her dish to the judges with only three minutes to spare. "I didn't know it," she says, "but my husband and the Pillsbury lady who was helping me were behind me having a heart attack—'Turn it in, turn it in!'"

Would Watts become a finalist in three consecutive Bake-Off Contests? Taking nothing for granted, she tried to come up with recipes between competitions, before the eligible ingredients were announced. "I was trying to think of some of the eligible products that might come into play—you know, give it three or four scenarios," says Watts, a former clothing-store manager who attributes her recipe-creating ability to "a pretty good imagination." That imagination got her into the next Bake-Off Contest as well, with her Macaroon–Peanut Butter–Chocolate Tartlets. On a base of Pillsbury refrigerated peanut butter cookie dough rolled in flaked coconut, a filling of peanut butter–chocolate mascarpone is topped with coconut-flavored mascarpone (see recipe, page 155).

Watts ended her Bake-Off career on a high note: The tartlets won her the Jif Peanut Butter Award, which came with a check for $5,000. But she says the best thing she took home from the competitions was new friendships. "Meeting everybody from all over the United States and finding the sweetest, most wonderful friends—I was just so blessed," she says. "And dancing with the Doughboy was just so much fun." She's glad she shared her grandmother's goal and persisted in pursuing it. "My grandma was right: You have to go for your dreams. You have to try, because life's just too precious."

Linda Drumm
Philadelphia

CONTEST 42 *Cinco de Mayo Glazed Chicken Wings*

Ask Linda Drumm how she became interested in cooking and baking, and she gives you a straight answer: "Well, I had to, with five young kids. I had to cook every day. We couldn't afford to go out." Her husband died of a heart attack at the age of 36, leaving her with the children and no income. To support her family, she took a job in automotive arbitration at the Better Business Bureau, where she met her second husband, Mike. "I really didn't love cooking until I met him," she says. "They say the way to a man's heart is through his stomach, so I worked my butt off for him."

Drumm describes Mike as "the most fantastic, wonderful, loving, kind, best-friend kind of guy," who not only helped raise her children but has also influenced her cooking. In fact, when she wanted to enter the Pillsbury Bake-Off Contest in 2006, after they'd been married 18 years, a conversation with Mike led to the recipe that got her in as a finalist. One evening, as the two drove from their jobs in Jackson Hole, Wyoming, to their home in Victor, Idaho, Drumm mentioned her recipe for glazed kebabs, which relied on lemon-lime soda for sweetness. Mike suggested she remake it with shrimp, but she replied that the shrimp would be overcooked by the time the soda thickened into a glaze. "He said, 'Why don't you try chicken wings and see if by the time the 7Up evaporates, they would be done enough?' They turned out perfect," she says. A few days after entering the recipe, she realized she'd omitted the serving size, so she resubmitted it—on May 5. Given the date and the Mexican-style eligible ingredients she used (Old El Paso green chiles and taco seasoning mix), Drumm renamed the dish Cinco de Mayo Glazed Chicken Wings. It was one of three recipes she entered in the 42nd Contest, and the Bake-Off team chose it as one of the 100 that would be competing.

After being selected as a finalist, Drumm became a local celebrity, interviewed by Idaho newspapers and television stations. "They made a big deal out of you, and you feel so good about yourself," she says. And then she was off to the Contest. "I loved it there, every part of it. They were so kind, the way they met you at the airport and shuttled you there. At the hotel, they gave us a bag of goodies."

Eating breakfast with the other finalists the morning of the Contest, Drumm was nervous about competing, but her butterflies disappeared when she was at her range and the band started playing "If I Had $1000000," by Barenaked Ladies. "I was cooking and smiling because I just kept singing inside my head," she says. A photograph from the 2006 Contest shows Drumm and the host, Joy Behar, sharing a hearty laugh.

The Pillsbury competition wasn't her first foray into the world of contests; Drumm started entering sweepstakes back when entries had to be mailed on 3-by-5-inch cards rather than submitted electronically. "I just kept winning and winning," she says, earning T-shirts, cash, cookware, cruises, and more. She moved on to baking contests, taking the top prize in *Country Living*'s Mom's Best Cake Contest (her entry: Nanny's Full o' Love Glazed Carrot Cake) and a host of local competitions in cities that she and Mike have called home, such as Broken Arrow, Oklahoma. "We've lived everywhere," she says, adding that she's become familiar with many types of American food as a result. But the cuisine she grew up with was on the other side of the Atlantic. Born in Grantham, a town in Lincolnshire, England, Drumm has a childhood memory of sitting on the kitchen counter while her father made pork pies, a regional specialty that consists of seasoned ground pork shoulder and pork jelly sealed in a hot-water-crust pie and eaten cold. "It's really delicious," she says.

With an open mind and a TV that's often tuned to the Food Network, Drumm is receptive to new culinary challenges. "I'm creative and I'm crazy and I'm impulsive and I'm positive," she says. She considers herself more of a cook than a baker, though she will bake for contests and family birthdays. Proud that her Cinco de Mayo Glazed Chicken Wings made it into one of the *Best of the Bake-Off* cookbooks, she encourages others to enter the Contest and advises them to pay attention to details—baking time, oven temperature, pan size, serving size—while they're testing recipes. "I know when I first started, I forgot to note, How long did I cook that for? So I had to start over," she says. Also, she adds, "ask questions if you need to and have fun."

Drumm entered the Pillsbury Bake-Off Contest for the second time in 2013, with seven recipes she knew wouldn't get in. She had been slacking off on entering competitions since 2010, when her oldest son died of a heart attack, just like his father. "I stopped doing those kinds of things," she says. "I wasn't super depressed, because I don't get depressed. I just gave up on a lot of things." But in the summer of 2016, a contest sponsored by Maple Leaf Farms piqued her interest, and she was back to thinking up recipes and testing them on Mike. "He's the greatest food critic ever—he loves everything I make!" she says.

For Drumm, the Bake-Off Contest was much more than a pleasant weekend. "It was one of the best experiences of my life," she says, from the moment she learned she was a finalist to the end of the competition. Did it change her at all, perhaps making her more confident or adventurous? "Not one bit," she says. "I'm always like that!"

▲ Mary Hawkes at Contest 37

▲ Lise Sullivan Ode, left, and Marie Bruno at Contest 46

◄ Heidi Givler at Contest 46

▲ Victoria Croce at Contest 47

▲ Marie Valdes and the Pillsbury Doughboy promote GE Appliances and the Bake-Off Contest at a Florida store before Contest 47.

▲ At Contest 47, from left, back row: Kim Van Dunk, Sindee Morgan, and Amy Siegel. Front row: Arlene Erlbach, Michele Kusma, and Susan Bickta, the administrator of a Facebook group for Bake-Off finalists and hopefuls.

▲ Brenda Watts at Contest 45

▼ Michele Kusma at Contest 46

▲ Shana Butler at Contest 47

▲ Pamela Shank at Contest 47

▼ Cathy Wiechert at Contest 46

▲ JoAnn Belack at Contest 44

◄ Laureen Pittman at Contest 44

▲ *Lesley Pew at Contest 46*

▲ *Kellie White at Contest 46*

▲ *Lise Sullivan Ode at Contest 46*

▲ Sindee Morgan at Contest 47

▲ Becky Pifer at Contest 45

▶ Mary Beth Protomastro at Contest 47

▲ Kroger supermarket wished Kim Rollings good luck with a giant billboard.

◄ Beth Royals shooting a video at Contest 47 after winning the sweets category. A month later, she won the grand prize.

▼ Anna Ginsberg and her daughter, Emma, then four, at Contest 42. Ginsberg won the grand prize, which will pay for Emma's college education.

For more photos, go to springformpress.com/gallery.

CHAPTER 4

Three Times and Out

IN 1979, Pillsbury instituted a rule: Three-time finalists are ineligible to enter future Pillsbury Bake-Off Contests. But oh what fun those finalists had reaching the limit! Cathy Wiechert, Laureen Pittman, and Pamela Shank tell how they got into the nation's most competitive baking contest the maximum number of times.

… SMART COOKIES

Cathy Wiechert
Hopkins, Minnesota

CONTEST 44 *Pecan Cookie Waffles With Honey-Cinnamon Butter*
CONTEST 46 *Orange Cardamom Blueberry Crostata*
CONTEST 47 *Lemon–Poppy Seed Pull-Apart Bread*

As a child, Cathy Wiechert was one up on the kids who appeared on the TV show *Romper Room,* which she watched faithfully. Every weekday, when the children on the program had their cookies at the appointed snack time, Cathy would run downstairs to her father's bakery and get herself a fresh chocolate doughnut. And not just a doughnut with chocolate glaze; a doughnut made from chocolate yeast dough, something you didn't see often in the 1960s.

Most people will never know the advantages of living above a bakery owned by their dad, but Wiechert knew them well. "The thing I remember most was I had free rein, so I kind of ran around the bakery," she says. Her early exposure to the baking business introduced her to the Pillsbury brand: Her father used to buy Pillsbury flour and sometimes put promotional Pillsbury items in the window display. "I remember he got one of the first Doughboys, the little Poppin' Fresh guy, for the showcase, which was kind of cool," Wiechert says. "Pillsbury was always in my memory."

As she grew up, some winning recipes from the Pillsbury Bake-Off Contest made an impression, such as the Chocolate Cherry Bars, devil's food squares baked with cherry pie filling. In college, her roommate's mother liked to make the Banana Crunch Cake, with its coconut-oat-pecan topping. Then, in 1996, when she was the mother of a toddler, Wiechert learned that the Bake-Off

Contest had just awarded its first million-dollar prize, for a Macadamia Fudge Torte. "I thought, I could do that," she says.

With the seven-figure prize in her sights, Wiechert submitted about 10 recipes in the next Contest, and another 10 or so in nearly every one until the Bake-Off team selected her Pecan Cookie Waffles With Honey-Cinnamon Butter in 2010. She hadn't even left for the competition when she had some Pillsbury success: In a monthly challenge the company sponsored before the Bake-Off Contest, Wiechert won $2,500 for her Pumpkin Snowballs, made with Pillsbury refrigerated sugar cookie dough and canned pumpkin.

Sugar cookie dough was also the main ingredient in her pecan waffles. "I was thinking about what went into the cookie dough, and I thought, Well, there's probably eggs and flour, things to make a batter," she says. After diluting the dough with half-and-half and two eggs, she was able to pour it into her waffle iron. Her daughter's boyfriend at the time taste-tested the waffles and quickly scarfed down four. "They're a little bit heavy because they're made out of cookie dough, and I think he got a stomachache afterward," she says. "But he really liked them, so I said, 'You know, I'll go ahead and enter them.'"

Wiechert's coworkers had done most of the taste testing for her entries, and they were so excited that she'd been named a finalist that they gave her a party, complete with a sheet cake decorated with the Bake-Off logo and the inscription GOOD LUCK CATHY! YOU'RE ONE IN A MILLION. They even chipped in cash "so I would have spending money down in Florida if I didn't win a million dollars," she says. "They were so supportive."

At the competition, she found her fellow finalists supportive, too. "Sometimes you watch the shows and you see people backstabbing," she says. "It's not really like that," at least at the Bake-Off Contest. Wiechert so enjoyed the camaraderie among people who shared her interest in baking and cooking that she resolved to return, and on the plane ride home she tried to think of recipes that would make that happen.

Wiechert's thought process for creating recipes isn't typical. "A lot of times I'll think of a name first," she says. If she likes the sound of it, she'll try to develop a recipe that fits it. Other times she aims to improve or simplify an existing dish. "The whole creative process" appeals to her, she says, and she likes to experiment. "When I was young, it wasn't the Easy-Bake Oven that I wanted," Wiechert explains. "That's what I got and I loved it, but what I really wanted for Christmas that year was a chemistry set. That just sounded like a lot of fun to me. I could mix things together and invent things." Even in her job as an accounts payable specialist, she most likes the creative aspect, "where I'm problem solving and trying to figure out where an issue is in an account or maybe where we're trying to match a credit to a debit and researching."

Her creativity and penchant for appealing names also got her into the 2013 and 2014 Contests, for her Orange Cardamom Blueberry Crostata and Lemon–Poppy Seed Pull-Apart Bread, respectively. With three Contests behind her, she's no longer eligible to participate, but that hasn't stopped the flow of Bake-Off ideas. "I'm thinking, Oh, what can I use this cookie dough with? or, What's the new flavor that's out there?" she says. She believes that coming up with original recipes is a bigger challenge now than ever: "With the internet, everything has been thought of. It's so hard." Her advice to Bake-Off hopefuls is to research how recipes are written so that if you do hit on a great idea, you can make yourself understood.

THREE TIMES AND OUT

Born and raised in neighboring Wisconsin, Wiechert lives near Minneapolis, home of the Pillsbury Bake-Off Contest's parent company. "I really like that General Mills is right here in town with us," she says. In 2015 a friend won a group trip to the company's test kitchens, and Wiechert was one of the lucky companions who got to visit the place where finalist recipes are vetted. "It was so much fun to actually see what went on in the kitchens," she says. Wiechert identified herself to the kitchen staff as a former finalist, and when she told them that her Contest 47 recipe was the Lemon–Poppy Seed Pull-Apart Bread, "they remembered it right away," she says. "They were excited to meet me, and I was excited to meet them."

The Minneapolis area is also home to a small community of former Bake-Off finalists, who meet for lunch every now and then. Someday they may be joined by another home cook who used to live above a bakery owned by her dad: Wiechert's sister, Gert. "She came with me to the last two Bake-Offs, and she just loved it," Wiechert says. "She loved meeting everyone, and she thought it was the most fun thing. So I know that when the next one comes up, she's going to try it herself."

Who wouldn't want to follow in Wiechert's footsteps? Since she first became a finalist, she has won contests sponsored by other companies, such as Chiquita. She started a popular blog, The Dutch Baker's Daughter (thedutchbakersdaughter.com), where she explains and illustrates recipes for dishes like Rhubarb Crumb Cake. And she continues to treasure "all the friendships that I've formed since the first time around," she says. The million-dollar prize may have motivated her to enter, but it was the experience that kept calling her back. "If I had won the million," she says, "that would have been the cherry on the cake."

though on the Food Network, she thought of her father, Hank Hubachek.

Laureen Pittman
Riverside, California

CONTEST 43 *Upside-Down Caramel-Apple Biscuits*
CONTEST 44 *Herb Chicken Sliders With Raspberry Mustard*
CONTEST 47 *Cheesy Cauliflower Tartlets*

Every time Laureen Pittman watched *Emeril Live* when it aired on the Food Network, she thought of her father, Hank Hubachek. Emeril Lagasse's outsize personality reminded her of Hubachek's, and the similarity didn't end there: Her dad was "a great cook," says Pittman, explaining that he got serious about his culinary hobby after retiring from his management job when she was a teen. "He was so creative in the kitchen," she says. "He really experimented."

Inspired by her father, Pittman became an adventurous cook herself, and in 2002, the year before Hubachek died, she entered a local contest sponsored by the Riverside County Orange Blossom Festival in Southern California. Her orange-and-chipotle shrimp dish won, and she liked way the contest scratched her competitive itch. "I thought, There's got to be more I could do, because it was fun for me, enjoying cooking so much and being able to compete with it," she says.

Not long afterward, Pittman came upon the website of Cooking Contest Central (cookingcontestcentral.com), which notifies its subscribers of cooking and baking competitions and provides forums for chatting and sharing information. "Once I found that website, I was amazed by this whole culture of competitive cooking and realized there was so much more out there," she says. At first she entered just the small contests she saw posted on the CCC site. "I thought the Pillsbury Bake-Off was beyond me," she says. "I thought, That's something I can't get into. That's the big one." But in 2006 she decided to take the plunge and entered a few recipes. None made it in, but she tried again in 2008. This time, "I surprised myself," she says. Of Pittman's three entries, the Bake-Off team selected one she had submitted in the dessert category: Upside-Down Caramel-Apple Cakes, in which Pillsbury biscuits are baked atop ramekins containing a mixture of apples, butter, caramel, and brown sugar. Even though the recipe featured biscuits, Pittman used the word *Cakes* in the title "because of all that sweetness I put on it, and once you turned it over and served it, it was more like dessert for me," she says. Pillsbury, however, went with a more literal interpretation, changing *Cakes* to *Biscuits* and moving the recipe to the breakfast category. Still, Pittman was a full-fledged finalist in her first Pillsbury Bake-Off Contest.

She got there, she says, by considering the biscuit the sum of its parts rather than the whole. "Instead of thinking, What could I do with a biscuit? I thought of it as, It's really just flour," she says. "Check the ingredients and think about what you could do with those instead of a biscuit." She also intentionally entered only a few recipes. "I don't like to go overboard with submitting a ton of recipes. I like to perfect just two or three and go with those," she explains. Her strategies worked: Pittman was a finalist in three of the six Bake-Off Contests she entered.

Her first finalist recipe may have been dessert-like, but Pittman says she's "not really a sweet cook," and her next two were on the savory side. For her Herb Chicken Sliders With Raspberry Mustard, she turned Pillsbury refrigerated crusty French loaf into small buns by slicing it and baking each piece in a muffin cup.

When her last Pillsbury competition opened for entries in 2014, she wanted to create an appetizer and decided to focus on one vegetable in particular: "Cauliflower was making a comeback in the vegetable world," she says. Seeing Green Giant Steamers Cauliflower & Cheese Sauce on the list of eligible ingredients, she thought of a tart she had made before, with caramelized onions, cauliflower, and cheese on puff pastry. "I kind of worked backwards" with the Green Giant product to create the Bake-Off version, she says. First, she caramelized onions, to which she added the cauliflower and cheese sauce, bacon, Parmesan cheese, and thyme. Then she divided the mixture among mini tart shells made from Pillsbury refrigerated pie crusts.

Pittman's husband, Guy, and their two sons are usually game to taste-test her creations, but Guy doesn't eat meat, so he'll sometimes have to pass up her contest entries. Occasionally she asks friends to try her dishes, and several of them have been inspired to enter the Bake-Off Contest themselves. "They haven't made it in, but I think it would be fun to get more people into this hobby," says Pittman, a paralegal turned writer whose forthcoming memoir, *The Lies That Bind*, chronicles her 30-year journey to find and connect with her biological family (she blogs about her journey at adoptionmytruth.com).

Pittman advises her friends and other Bake-Off hopefuls to avoid complicated dishes. "In some contests, they want really elaborate, fancy stuff, but Pillsbury likes to keep it simple," she says. That was especially true when the company limited the number of ingredients in Contests 46 and 47—a change that Pittman liked. "I think it made it easier," she says. "As a creative cook, you tend to maybe add something else, an element that you think is going to set it apart, and maybe you're never finished in your mind. But when you limit the number of ingredients, it kind of takes the burden off: Well, I can only use seven ingredients. How am I going to get the best bang for my buck?"

Although she was first enticed by the creative challenge and the grand prize, what Pittman most enjoyed about the Pillsbury Bake-Off Contest was the atmosphere—"the camaraderie and the meeting people and just the event itself," she says. She now has a network of cooking buddies across the country whom she met at the Bake-Off Contest or another competition, such as the World Food Championships. Once a year she gets together with four of them, including Beth Royals, who won the 47th Pillsbury Bake-Off Contest (see page 126).

Of the many contests Pittman has participated in over the years, several stand out: High Liner Foods' Fisher Boy awarded her $10,000; Star Olive Oils gave her a culinary vacation in Spain. At the Food Network's *Ultimate Recipe Showdown*, she felt honored to cook in the company's kitchens. With broad experience in contests, she has her favorites. "One of the best cooking adventures I've ever had was the Pillsbury Bake-Off," Pittman says. "Once you get there one time, you want to go back. It was so much fun."

Pamela Shank
Parkersburg, West Virginia

CONTEST 43 *Mascarpone-Filled Cranberry-Walnut Rolls*
CONTEST 44 *Peanut Butter–Toffee Cheesecake Brownies*
CONTEST 47 *Strawberry-Mascarpone-Hazelnut Chocolate Tart*

Pamela Shank's mother couldn't afford to buy magazines when Pam was a child, but she always found the money to buy the recipe magazines that appeared in supermarket checkout racks after the Pillsbury Bake-Off Contests were held. "I remember how excited my mother was when the Bake-Off cookbook came out each time," Shank says. "We would sit and look through them, and she would make so many of the recipes. We always talked about the dream of being one of those ladies" who became finalists. But neither mother nor daughter entered the Bake-Off Contest, figuring that it wasn't intended for them. "We thought it was always somebody in the big cities or somebody farther away," says Shank, a lifelong West Virginian.

Fast-forward to 2006, and Shank, by now a grandmother, is watching highlights of the Pillsbury Bake-Off Contest on TV. "I thought, Gosh, it looks like they're normal people," she says. "So maybe somewhere down the road I might get brave enough to try that." Two years later, she summoned her bravery, and with her seven-year-old granddaughter's help, she created Mascarpone-Filled Cranberry-Walnut Rolls from Pillsbury refrigerated biscuits. "We were making monkey bread, and it just kind of evolved," Shank says. The Bake-Off team selected the rolls as one of the 100 finalist recipes in the 43rd Contest, and Shank was set to compete in the event that had long fascinated her mother, four years after she died.

Even though her mother's high regard for the early Bake-Off recipes was a vivid memory, Shank wasn't nervous at the competition. "Everything seemed really smooth and easy," she says. She wasn't even thrown off when a reporter walking the Contest floor asked her, "How does a person who lives in West Virginia know anything about mascarpone cheese?" "I thought, I don't know how to take that," she says. "Of course, I was so excited to be there, nothing was going to bring me down." But her calm demeanor dissolved at the awards ceremony when her Mascarpone-Filled Cranberry-Walnut Rolls won the breakfast/brunch category. Called to the stage, Shank told the host, Sandra Lee, that she was having "an out-of-body experience."

"I was shaking so badly," Shank recalls. Winning the category earned her $5,000 and a range and also gave her a 1-in-4 shot at the million-dollar grand prize. After an interviewer asked her, "Why should your recipe be the million-dollar winner today?" Shank, whose modesty is matched by her admiration for her fellow finalists, replied, "My recipe is no better than everybody else's in this room. Anybody could be up here winning this million." The grand prize went to Carolyn Gurtz of Gaithersburg, Maryland, for her Double-Delight Peanut Butter Cookies.

Nonetheless, Shank's place in the Contest's history is cemented with her category win and two more finalist turns, for her Peanut Butter–Toffee Cheesecake Brownies in 2010 and her Strawberry-Mascarpone-Hazelnut Chocolate Tart in 2014. She entered a total of five Bake-Off Contests and submitted seven to 11 recipes in each.

Her methods of creating her Pillsbury entries varied, though they all began the same way. "I started with the taste first," Shank says, "and then tried to form [the ingredients] into something that looked like it was going to hold together." For inspiration she would read *Food Network Magazine*, watch Paula Deen and Trisha Yearwood on the Food Network, and peruse old cookbooks, trying "to think of ways to adjust recipes to be a little more modern." She also looked through her mother's old scratch recipes with an eye toward re-creating them with Pillsbury products. Then, too, she sometimes walked through the supermarket, especially in the frozen-food aisle, with the goal of finding a dish she could improve on. Shank likes to try new ingredients and thinks unusual ones catch the Bake-Off team's attention, but she also cautions contestants, "You want to keep it that anybody could buy it at the grocery store. The average person doesn't want to go spending $20 for this tiny bottle of something to use a half teaspoon of it."

How does all that translate into a recipe? Shank describes how she created her Strawberry-Mascarpone-Hazelnut Chocolate Tart: "I stood in front of my pantry, and I just pulled out everything that was on the Pillsbury list that I had. Then I bought a couple more things at the grocery store, like white melting chocolate, and I just kind of started moving things around on the counter to see what might go together. And that's how I ended up with the hazelnut chocolate spread with the white chocolate; those two things tasted awesome together. And so then I thought, Well, strawberries would go well with that. So I kind of formed it just by putting the ingredients together and trying to think of what to make with it. Kind of a backwards way, isn't it?"

To chronicle her experiences in the Bake-Off Contest, Shank has compiled scrapbooks. "I hope that someday one of my kids or grandkids will look through those and will feel the excitement I felt for it," she says. She has also published some details on her blog, Grandma Honey's House (grandmahoneyshouse.com); she's Grandma Honey to her 14 grandchildren, who have taste-tested her recipes, including her Bake-Off entries. Their honest appraisals have helped her win awards from companies and magazines such as Martha White, *Family Circle*, and *EatingWell*.

Shank hasn't been entering many contests in recent years, even though she retired in 2015, after 42 years as a registered nurse. Instead, she's learning about blogging by watching videos and reading online tutorials. Her blog has a section called Kids' Cooking Classes, where she describes the baking or cooking lessons she has given her grandchildren, who appear in the step-by-step photographs. "They all love to bake and cook and want to go to a Bake-Off also," she says. "They were so proud of me the times I did get to attend."

That pride had nothing to do with whether she took home a prize. "I truly think you already won when you were chosen to go," Shank says. Asked what aspect of her personality helped her get into the exclusive club of three-time Pillsbury Bake-Off finalists, she says, "I think that part of me is my mother coming through.... I always felt that she was with me through this adventure. I only wish she really could have been."

See also Mary Hawkes (page 14), Arlene Erlbach (page 28), Brenda Watts (page 55), and Beth Royals (page 126).

CHAPTER 5

Last Dance With the Doughboy

UNLESS GENERAL MILLS changes the 1979 eligibility rule, home cooks who have competed in the Pillsbury Bake-Off Contest twice have only one more chance to be finalists. Does that affect their approach to the Contest? Find out from Kim Van Dunk, JoAnn Belack, Kellie White, Amy Siegel, Lise Sullivan Ode, and Sindee Morgan.

Kim Van Dunk
Caldwell, New Jersey

CONTEST 46 *Meatball and Breadstick Sub Skewers*
CONTEST 47 *Banana–Chocolate Chip Streusel Muffins*

Google "Meatball and Breadstick Sub Skewers," and you'll see Kim Van Dunk's recipe all over the internet—on Pinterest, YouTube, food blogs, websites. The name and ingredients are sometimes changed a bit, and often there's no mention that the recipe originated with Van Dunk and the 46th Pillsbury Bake-Off Contest. But that's the nature of the most innovative Bake-Off recipes: They're copied ad infinitum. Like the French Silk Chocolate Pie of Contest 3 and the Tunnel of Fudge Cake of Contest 17, Van Dunk's Meatball and Breadstick Sub Skewers are frequently made by home cooks across the country who have no idea that the recipe was the brainchild of a Pillsbury Bake-Off finalist.

The meatball skewers were Van Dunk's first recipe to be accepted into the Bake-Off Contest but her second attempt; her first entry, in Contest 45, was so forgettable that even she doesn't remember what it was. "I just thought if you sent in a good recipe, you had a shot," she says. "I didn't really understand that whole behind-the-scenes process there is for researching and trying to come up with something creative." When she started entering other cooking competitions, she learned more.

Since the 46th Pillsbury Bake-Off Contest opened, Van Dunk has followed a method: She first reviews previous Bake-Off recipes, and then, when she has an idea, she searches for it on the Pillsbury website (pillsbury.com). "I plug in my ideas and see if they're already there, and if they are, it's probably something I'll steer away from," she says. "My whole mentality and my whole thought process about Pillsbury is to do something that's not on their site, that's not on the radar for them, because I think that will set your recipe apart from that whole huge pool of everybody else."

Her new approach worked right away. "I remember seeing a recipe from one of the past Bake-Offs that was a skewer-type recipe and thinking, Wow, I haven't seen that anywhere else on any of these other Bake-Off lists," she says. She then searched pillsbury.com and found few skewer recipes there. "That kind of got me thinking," she says. On her blog, Life in the Van (lifeinthevan.com), she describes what happened next:

> One evening, while I was rolling out miniature meatballs to pop into a pot of soup, it hit me. My kids love these little meatballs. I bet they'd love them more on skewers, maybe with a breadstick twisted around them, with cheese and a dipping sauce. I had an image in my head of what the finished product would ideally look like, but I wasn't sure if it would all come together. My kids were busy playing outside so I took the opportunity to give my recipe a try. I remember holding my breath when I opened the oven door and exclaiming, "It worked."

Even better, when Van Dunk searched the internet for a meatball-and-breadstick skewer recipe, she came up empty. "That recipe was nowhere to be found—nowhere," she says. "That's when I knew that it was the recipe I wanted to perfect and tweak. It hadn't been done before, and I knew it would stand out." Van Dunk's Meatball and Breadstick Sub Skewers received considerable media attention before and during the Bake-Off Contest, but the grand prize went to Glori Spriggs of Henderson, Nevada, for her Loaded Potato Pinwheels. "The winner had a great idea, and it was really very easy to execute," Van Dunk says. "I remember watching her do a demonstration on TV, and it was pretty simple. Anybody could make it." Van Dunk couldn't help comparing her recipe with Spriggs's. "I kind of looked at my meatball recipe, and I still love it and I thought it was really creative, but it was definitely something that not everybody would attempt to make," she says. "For me, making homemade meatballs is no big deal—I do it all the time—but not everybody may want to spend the time making 36 little meatballs and placing them all on skewers and weaving them through breadsticks."

With the Loaded Potato Pinwheels in mind, Van Dunk created 10 easy recipes for Contest 47 in 2014, and the Bake-Off team selected her Banana–Chocolate Chip Streusel Muffins, made from Pillsbury Gluten Free refrigerated chocolate chip cookie dough. "When they picked my little muffin, I knew automatically I was not coming home with a prize," she says. Surprised by the choice, she says that "there was really nothing that made it stand out"—and that she thought one or two of her other entries had greater potential. "I was grateful to go and loved my experience there, but I didn't expect to win anything," she says. And she didn't.

Looking back on all 10 of her easy entries in the 47th Bake-Off Contest, Van Dunk says they were "so not me." What was? Her widely copied and distributed skewer recipe. "I realize now if we get another opportunity to try for a third attempt, I would probably go back to my original thinking that I had when I made those meatball skewers," says Van Dunk, a self-taught cook who subscribes to *EatingWell* and *Cook's Illustrated* magazines. "That recipe was totally me, and you have to make a recipe that reflects you, that you stand behind. I won't shy away from something that requires a little bit of labor, because that's how I cook.... I'll stick with what works for me, and if it works for the judges, then that's great."

Following her instincts has gotten Van Dunk far in the world of competitive cooking: She has a long résumé of prizes and honors from companies and magazines such as Eggland's Best, Tyson Foods, Rodelle, *Cook's Country*, *Good Housekeeping*, and *Organic Gardening*, and she's been featured in *Better Homes and Gardens*, *Taste of Home*, and *Country Woman*. Her husband and three sons often help with the taste testing, though food allergies and celiac disease sometimes prevent the kids from trying her creations. She's glad her boys have had a front-row seat to her contesting. "I try to hit home with my kids that if you want to try to win something, you also have to be willing to lose, and you have to be OK with that," says Van Dunk, a former elementary-school teacher who has homeschooled her sons. The entire family saw a lot of winning and losing firsthand after driving from their New Jersey home to Nashville for the 47th Pillsbury Bake-Off Contest. The competition impressed Van Dunk's oldest son, then 14, so much that he told her he wanted to enter when he was old enough. "I think that's kind of cool," she says.

The family didn't accompany Van Dunk to the 46th Bake-Off Contest, held the previous year in Las Vegas, so she traveled solo—for the first time. Finding the experience "empowering," she came away with a solid appreciation for the opportunities Pillsbury provides to "people who might not have the chance to do these things," she says. "A lot of people who enter are just living their normal lives—they're working a job or a stay-at-home mom or whatnot, and oftentimes they're selfless and wouldn't think to do something like this for themselves. I love the fact that Pillsbury takes the time to praise people who ordinarily don't get any recognition and don't seek it either."

If Van Dunk enters the Pillsbury Bake-Off Contest again, she'll be mindful of the fact that she has just one finalist turn left unless the rules change. "I will only enter a recipe that I really feel has the potential to win something," she says. "Probably only one or two recipes. I wouldn't just casually enter an idea." Having seen her muffins edge out her other entries, she wants to be certain that her next finalist recipe has "a creative and unique look to it, takes some kind of classic idea but turns it on its head, and gets people's attention a bit." Even so, she isn't single-mindedly focused on winning, as she was when she first became a finalist. "I didn't get what everybody else felt about the Bake-Off," she says. On the internet, "you hear all this back-and-forth chatter about it, and you see all the excitement, but it was really foreign to me. I couldn't quite wrap my arms around it. But after going, you get it."

JoAnn Belack
Bradenton, Florida

CONTEST 44 *"Mamma Mia" Ravioli Bites*

CONTEST 47 *Pepper Jack–Salsa Flatbread With an Italian Twist*

As JoAnn Belack sees it, she made her way into the Pillsbury Bake-Off Contest not just by being a smart cookie but by being a tough cookie, too.

Belack says you need a thick skin even before you submit recipes, because getting candid feedback on your dishes from friends and family is vital. For Contest 47, she held a taste testing on a day when she had prepared five recipes. "I called in all the neighbors, and we sat around the dining room table. I said, 'I want you to be brutal. Tell me what you don't like and what you do like. I have no ego about this,'" she says. "If your feelings get hurt by criticism, then this hobby is not for you."

A thick skin is also helpful if the competition involves voting. In Contests 45 and 46, General Mills put semifinalist recipes up for an internet vote, and the public decided which of them became finalists. Belack had a semifinalist recipe in each Contest—her Italian Brunch Strata in the 45th and her Chewy Ginger Date Granola Bars in the 46th—and says she did "tremendous public relations" to get votes, including walking around for weeks in an orange T-shirt printed with voting information. Despite her efforts, she lost both times. "It was devastating to get so close and do so much work and then to lose," she says.

But this tough cookie persevered, and when Contest 47 opened in 2014, she again entered, with her usual number of recipes—about

26. The Bake-Off team chose her Pepper Jack–Salsa Flatbread With an Italian Twist as a finalist recipe; there were no semifinalists. Like Contest 44, in which Belack competed with her "Mamma Mia" Ravioli Bites, Contest 47 didn't require participants to receive votes before moving on to become finalists.

That means Belack was a finalist or semifinalist in four consecutive Bake-Off Contests. Clearly she was doing something right, but she didn't always have so much success. In fact, it took Belack from the mid-1990s until 2010 to catch Pillsbury's attention with her entries. "Eventually I figured it out," she says. "In the beginning, when I was trying all those years, I was entering recipes that were so complicated. They weren't simple enough. Finally, just by studying the entries that were on the internet from previous years, I realized, You need to rethink your approach to this whole thing."

Reviewing recipes on pillsbury.com, Belack concluded, "Pillsbury has streamlined the Bake-Off recipes to the way people cook today. People want to make something fast and easy and with few ingredients, but it still has to taste great and look great."

Once a Bake-Off Contest opens and Belack decides to commit to it, she's all in. "I'm thinking about it 24/7," she says. With notebooks stashed everywhere—in the kitchen, next to her bed, on her desk, in the car—she's ready to jot down ideas before they flee her mind, and she has even scribbled several at red lights. Belack often calls on her Italian heritage but doesn't rely on it: "Absolutely put in a lot of what you know, but you've got to branch out and cover other areas." For her Pepper Jack–Salsa Flatbread With an Italian Twist, she combined two ethnic dishes.

Belack's memories of growing up in a large Italian-American family in South Orange, New Jersey, center on food. "My grandparents, who immigrated to the United States from Naples, Italy, in the early 1900s, were amazing cooks," she says. "To this day, I have never tasted Italian cooking equal to theirs." She remembers watching her grandfather toss food in a sauté pan, with flames shooting up high. And her grandmother? "She always chopped parsley with a cleaver at lightning speed," Belack says.

The emphasis on good food made a discerning diner out of Belack at an early age, and relatives recall her ordering lobster fra diavolo at a restaurant when she was a toddler. But she didn't start cooking until she was in college and part of a group of friends who took turns preparing meals based on their ethnic heritage. "Suddenly I was making everything, and I was really a good cook," she says. "And I loved cooking!"

After graduating with a degree in pottery ("I always say, 'It was the '60s'") and moving to Florida, Belack put her time and energy into her art, starting a wholesale business and making all the pots and planters herself. Eventually her wrists gave out, and she moved on to other work, running a resort-wear boutique, selling a line of jewelry and accessories, and fund-raising for an educational foundation.

Along the way, Belack was aware of the Pillsbury Bake-Off Contest and other cooking competitions but didn't know much about them. Then she came across the book *Cookoff: Recipe Fever in America*, by Amy Sutherland, and read it in one night. Intrigued by Sutherland's tales of the cooking-contest world, Belack found her way to the website of Cooking Contest Central (cookingcontest central.com), with its lists of competitions and forums for subscribers. "A few small wins started an obsession," she says. "I just wish I knew about all this when I was a lot younger."

Once she became a finalist in her first Pillsbury Bake-Off Contest, Belack was exposed to another world, too: that of the television interview. She appeared on two Florida shows as well as Fox News, which sent the host and a crew to her kitchen. "I'm a very outgoing person, an extrovert, so it was really fun for me," she says.

With only one more chance left to participate in the Bake-Off Contest unless the rules change, Belack doesn't plan to adjust her latest methods. "I'll just keep doing what I've been doing unless there's some whole new parameter out there that you have to figure out," she says. She'll follow the same advice she gives others:

- "Just be flexible as to whatever the rules are," she says. And read the rules "a million times."
- Keep your recipe "very simple, very tasty, and very quick. I think that's kind of it in a nutshell," says Belack, who subscribes to about 10 food magazines, including *Saveur* and *Food & Wine*. "But it can't be that ordinary, because there are more people and more ethnic groups in there now, and they are all using their cultural heritage, which is great for the variety. I think you need to be aware of what's going on in other cuisines."
- Don't get "too emotionally invested" in the recipes you submit. "The point is to get chosen and to do what is needed to be chosen," she says.

Having been tapped four times in a row, "I can't even imagine being chosen" for a fifth consecutive time, Belack says. "The odds are stacked against me for the next one, but I'll still give it my all." She continues to recommend the Bake-Off Contest to others: "It will be one of the highlights of your life, an accomplishment you can be so proud of.... I am even going to mention it in my obituary!"

LAST DANCE WITH THE DOUGHBOY

Kellie White
St. Louis

CONTEST 44 *Zesty Lime-Fish Tacos*
CONTEST 46 *Honey Sesame Bagels*

When the 47th Pillsbury Bake-Off Contest opened in 2014, Kellie White tried her darndest to come up with a recipe that wouldn't just get her in as a finalist but would also have a good shot at the million-dollar grand prize. Having been a finalist twice before—in 2010, with her Zesty Lime-Fish Tacos, and in 2013, with her Honey Sesame Bagels—she had only one more opportunity to compete at the event. Determining that none of her 2014 ideas were million-dollar contenders, she made a bold decision: She wouldn't enter Contest 47 at all. "I don't want to just go; I want to go and win it!" she says with a laugh.

White's motive had changed since she first entered the competition. Initially, she simply wanted to become part of "such an iconic contest," she says. "I had never entered a cooking contest before, and it seemed like it would be so much fun." Her first Bake-Off Contest wound up being more than fun; it put the million-dollar award within her grasp. Her Zesty Lime-Fish Tacos won the dinner category, giving her a 1-in-4 chance of taking home the grand prize.

White describes what happened when her fish tacos nabbed the Dinners Made Easy title: "The whole thing was really exciting, because when they announced the category winners, we knew that [we] would be going to [*The Oprah Winfrey Show*]. They whisked us off the stage and took us into a pressroom. We sat at a table, and the press interviewed us, and then we were sent to get our bags.

A limo met us outside and took us to the airport, and we flew in the Pillsbury private jet to Chicago that night." There was a day for shopping. "They gave us an allowance, and we bought clothes for the show," White explains. "There was a lot of scrutiny over what people were going to wear."

The grand prize went to Sue Compton of Delanco, New Jersey, for her Mini Ice Cream Cookie Cups, but White left the show with a sharper focus on winning a Bake-Off Contest. Three years and two contests later, she was again a finalist, with her Honey Sesame Bagels. Like her fish tacos, it won a prize—this time, the GE Imagination at Work Award, for which she received $5,000 worth of GE appliances. (The fish tacos had earned her $5,000 and a range.)

What was it about the two recipes that not only got White into the Bake-Off Contest but also won awards? "I think it's that the recipes did something different with the Pillsbury ingredients that hadn't been done before, and I think they like that," she says. For her Zesty Lime-Fish Tacos, she made taco shells from biscuits, and for her Honey Sesame Bagels, she made bagels out of pizza dough. "As far as I know, those were pretty unique uses of their products," says White, who adds that she enjoyed demonstrating both recipes on local TV shows.

White gives considerable thought to each Bake-Off recipe she enters. Once the rules are announced, "I'll go and buy a whole bunch of Pillsbury products and some other basic ingredients," she says, "and just sit and look at them and try to think of some things to do with them. I usually test a whole bunch of recipes in a weekend." For taste testing, White says she relies on her husband "and the kids if they're willing to eat it." She has entered two or three recipes in each of three Bake-Off Contests.

Unlike some other finalists, White doesn't spend time thinking of ideas between the competitions. "I like to see what the sponsor ingredients are, because that can inspire what I do," she says. She did, however, start entering other cooking contests in the intervening years. In 2014, White won the #TopTater Recipe Contest and competed in the World Food Championships, and two years later she placed in the Bubba Burger contest. "I'm always thinking about new recipes for different contests," she says.

White has been baking from a young age, graduating from an Easy-Bake Oven to a real one when she was seven years old. She remembers her first baked dish: a butterscotch cake. "I'm pretty sure it was terrible," she says, "but my parents swore it was delicious." Years later she became interested in cooking, influenced by her mother and other relatives. "My mom always made home-cooked meals, and her side of the family is from the South," she says. "There were some great Southern cooks in that group," including White's grandmother. "I also have to give a lot of credit to the Food Network, which inspires home cooks like me to expand our cooking skills and repertoire. I get a lot of ideas from watching Food Network." In particular, she likes *Barefoot Contessa* as well as shows like *Chopped*, "where they have to come up with something on the fly," she says. "I think they're very creative." She also subscribes to food magazines such as *Cook's Illustrated*, *Bon Appétit*, and *Saveur*.

"I enjoy coming up with new ideas, whether it's at work or in the kitchen," says White, an acquisitions editor at the medical publishing house Elsevier, where she shepherds books through development and production. Indeed, one of her colleagues wrote on LinkedIn, "When I need help 'thinking outside the box,' Kellie is my go-to source."

Sometimes when White learns that a coworker enjoys cooking or baking, she recommends the Pillsbury Bake-Off Contest. "Basically, anybody can do it," she says. "When I started entering, I never really thought my recipe would be accepted. Now I've been twice. I think you just can't discount yourself. Anybody can have a great idea." Even though she's aiming for the grand prize, her favorite aspect of the Contest has been meeting all the other home cooks. "It's really so much fun," she says. "I've made so many great friends that will be lifelong friends. Now any time I go to these cooking contests, it's kind of like a little reunion."

Amy Siegel
Clifton, New Jersey

CONTEST 45 *Strawberry Swirl–Peanut Butter–Brownie Cupcakes*
CONTEST 47 *Sesame Mini Pitas With Roasted Red Pepper Tapenade*

The Pillsbury Bake-Off Contest is by no means a no-holds-barred competition. There are lists of qualifying products, eligibility requirements for participants, and, in recent years, rules about the number of ingredients and the length of the prep time in recipes. But restrictions don't scare Amy Siegel: She cooks and bakes for one daughter who has food allergies, another who has celiac disease, and an entire family that keeps kosher.

Siegel has managed to become a finalist twice without using a single tube in Pillsbury's time-honored line of refrigerated dough products—no biscuits, Crescent rolls, breadsticks, cookie dough, crusty French loaf, cinnamon rolls, or pizza dough. "None of those are kosher," she says. For her Strawberry Swirl–Peanut Butter–Brownie Cupcakes, which got her into her first Bake-Off Contest, she used Pillsbury brownie mix, a kosher product that was an eligible ingredient that year. The cupcake recipe "came out of trying to figure out how I could use the brownie mix not as a brownie mix," she says. "And I happened to have a really good cream cheese frosting that I like to make, so those two things came together." Siegel also tried to incorporate as many sponsor products as possible, including Jif Peanut Butter and Smucker's Strawberry Jam, so she'd be eligible for more prizes. The result was a cupcake that "really tasted like a PBJ sandwich," in the words of one reviewer on pillsbury.com.

Siegel didn't win a prize, but instead of getting discouraged, she did her homework. "Once I got in the first time, I started to analyze things that they were looking for," she says. "I just sort of tried to study the winning recipes more and figure out what the winning formulas were, if there were any." In the next Contest, number 46, her Jalapeño Cheddar Muffins With Peach Filling were chosen as a semifinalist recipe, but they didn't receive enough online votes to make her a finalist.

When the eligible products for the 47th Bake-Off Contest were announced in 2014, Siegel immediately knew she could bake in her comfort zone. On the list was Pillsbury's new line of gluten-free products: tubs of cookie dough, pizza crust dough, and pie and pastry dough, all of it kosher and safe for her daughter who has celiac disease. With a good understanding of gluten-free baking—Siegel even writes a blog called The Gluten-Free Maven (theglutenfreemaven.com)—"I felt like I knew the products really well," she says. The new line opened up Bake-Off possibilities for Siegel, whose restrictions had kept her focused on desserts since she started entering recipes consistently in 2004. "Once there was a gluten-free pizza and pie crust, I was able to do more savory stuff," she says. She tripled the number of recipes she ordinarily entered, to more than three dozen, and the Bake-Off team selected her Sesame Mini Pitas With Roasted Red Pepper Tapenade, made with Pillsbury Gluten Free refrigerated pizza crust dough. For the second time, she competed in the Pillsbury Bake-Off Contest.

Siegel says she was surprised that both her cupcakes and her pitas were chosen over her other entries. "I had other recipes that were my favorites," she says. But she can see why the Bake-Off team selected them: In 2012, cupcakes were "still pretty hot," she says, and her recipe used five sponsor products. In 2014, Pillsbury had just launched its line of gluten-free products, "so I sort of played to that," she says. (Pillsbury has since discontinued the line.)

Whether her recipe is for a sweet or savory dish, Siegel starts writing it down "right from the beginning," she says. "I almost approach it like you would do a lab in science class. I first put the idea on paper, and then I start fiddling, but I try to keep notes because sometimes you want to go back." If a Bake-Off idea occurs to her between Contests, before the eligible products are announced, she'll write a short email message, type "PBO" in the subject line, and send it off—to herself. "When the Contest comes out, I just compile everything into a list and see if I want to actually try any of them," she says.

What makes Siegel adept at creating recipes? "I'm very adventurous with food," she says, "and I think I have a good palate. I can remember something I ate a long time ago in a restaurant." She also has a knack for balancing spices. Then, too, developing recipes "happens to click as a creative outlet," she says. Since becoming a finalist the first time, she has encouraged others to enter the Bake-Off Contest: "I say, 'You're not losing anything. There's no entrance fee. Experiment with what you like; you can eat for dinner whatever you're making, so it's not a financial loss, as with other crafts.'"

Siegel may or may not shift her strategy for her last chance at becoming a finalist. "You sort of have to adapt" to the rules for each Bake-Off Contest, she says, because they always change. "Otherwise I think a good strategy is to use as many sponsor products as you can and to follow trends so you can see what is currently appealing to the American people." One way Siegel stays up-to-date with food trends is by reading restaurant reviews in her local New Jersey newspaper. She also reads magazines such as *Bon Appétit, Cook's Country,* and *Gluten Free & More* and watches TV shows such as *Cupcake Wars, Chopped,* and "pretty much any of the Gordon Ramsay ones." ("I don't really like him necessarily," she says. "I just like that they have amateur cooks.")

Siegel has been watching cooking shows since they were largely the purview of PBS and she was a child eager to learn baking skills. "Both my mother and grandmother were good cooks, but they weren't into baking, so I naturally took that over," she says. When she was 10 years old, she started an annual tradition of making an assortment of pies for Thanksgiving, and she entered a recipe contest sponsored by her local newspaper, *Newsday,* of Long Island, New York. Her entry: Strawberry Birthday Cake. "They had a 'Kids in the Kitchen' section, and it was published, and I was very excited," she says. "It sort of went from there." Siegel entered a single Pillsbury Bake-Off Contest in her teens, didn't get in, and dropped the idea. But the first year she was married, she decided to give contesting another shot and entered a competition sponsored by Kraft. Her Festive Eggnog Cake won the grand prize, even though she hadn't tested it first. "I just sort of did it in my head," she says, "and then when I won, I Googled around to see what other contests there were." She started entering competitions regularly, and in 2009 she took first place in the Simply Manischewitz Cook-Off with her Marvelous Mediterranean Falafel Sliders.

Since giving birth to a fourth daughter, Siegel hasn't had much time for contests. She has also lost some interest, now that more cooking competitions are requiring contestants to submit videos and photos. "It's not so much about the recipe as how you sell it," she says. Regardless of what the future holds for cooking competitions, the Bake-Off Contest will always be a special memory for Siegel. "That whole community and the whole experience of being chosen out of a large pool of people, I really viewed it as a privilege," she says. "'We're just happy to be here'—that's sort of the way you feel." There was a bonus, too: "It was a nice break for me as a mother of young children to go away without them for a little bit and also to be with people who really understood what your passion is."

Lise Sullivan Ode
Cumming, Georgia

CONTEST 46 *German Chocolate Doughnuts*
CONTEST 47 *Lemon-Blueberry Muffins*

Lise Sullivan Ode isn't just a two-time Pillsbury Bake-Off finalist; she's a two-time finalist who, on her own, prepared all the grand-prize-winning recipes in the Bake-Off Contest's history. And yet there was a point where she turned away from the competition.

That period began in 2004, after Ode entered the Bake-Off Contest for the first time, with three recipes she'd fussed over. None were chosen. "It must be impossible to get into this contest," she remembers thinking. "I don't want to spend lots of time on something that's never going to happen." So she put the competition out of her mind.

Nine years later, while visiting a coupon website, Ode was offered a $5 gift card from Kroger supermarket in exchange for one task: enter a recipe in the Pillsbury Bake-Off Contest. She quickly sent a recipe without testing it, received her gift card—and found herself giving the Contest more thought. "I just got the idea in my head, Well, maybe I'll try it," she says. So she began developing recipes, reworking them until they met her standards and Pillsbury's requirements. "I started thinking, Am I crazy? What am I doing? I'm spending a lot of money. But I just thought, I'm in it now. I'm committed to it," says Ode, who has been baking since childhood.

By the deadline, she had entered five recipes, and one stood out. "I was really excited about the German Chocolate Doughnuts," she says. "I was trying to come up with something completely original, that no one had ever done. That was the one thing that when I Googled it, nothing came up. I thought, Maybe I'm on to something."

The doughnuts were creative on at least two levels: They combined two desserts—German chocolate cake and doughnuts—and they repurposed an eligible product, Pillsbury Grands! Flaky Layers refrigerated Honey Butter biscuits. They also had a sentimental connection for Ode, given that her father, who had died earlier that year, loved German chocolate cake. But while Ode felt that the recipe was "good enough to be in the Contest," she knew from experience that the number of entries Pillsbury received left her with a minute chance of getting in.

This time Ode defied the odds, and when the Bake-Off team notified her that she would be competing in the 46th Pillsbury Bake-Off Contest—with her German Chocolate Doughnuts—she was "thrilled," she says. "It was really very, very exciting." The Contest itself offered its own excitement. "I loved making new friends and meeting lots of people who shared a baking passion," says Ode. But she had an even bigger takeaway: "I realized I really enjoyed creating recipes." For Ode, a former graphic designer at the *National Enquirer* and a photography enthusiast, the next step came naturally. She started a blog, Mom Loves Baking (momlovesbaking.com), where she explains her original recipes and posts step-by-step photos, and sometimes videos, of her baked goods in the making.

One of the first challenges Ode assigned herself on Mom Loves Baking was to prepare every grand-prize-winning Pillsbury Bake-Off recipe within a year—53 in all, once she added the 2014 winner. After completing the project, with no time to spare, Ode had a rare overview of the winning recipes. She noticed, for instance, that some of the early ones "taste good but don't look great in pictures," she says, suggesting that appearance has played a bigger role in the later Bake-Off Contests. She also had her favorites: Snappy Turtle Cookies (1952), Spicy Apple Twists (1958), Chocolate Cherry Bars (1974), Chocolate Praline Layer Cake (1988), Fudgy Bonbons (1994), and the 2014 winner, Peanutty Pie Crust Clusters. For Ode's blog posts on all 53 recipes, go to momlovesbaking.com/baking-project.

Ode competed against the Peanutty Pie Crust Clusters in the 2014 Contest with her Lemon-Blueberry Muffins. "Something I learned between 2013 and 2014 is that I initially thought you had to have a completely original recipe that had never been done before by anyone in the world" in order to become a finalist, she says. Michele Kusma's Blueberry Sour Cream Pancakes, a finalist recipe in 2013 (see page 47), changed her thinking. "Pancakes are not an original recipe, but it's original because she made pancakes out of cookie dough," Ode says. "I learned that by being in [the Contest], and I thought, OK, that opens up a whole new world."

Ode put her new lesson into practice when she created her 11 entries for the 2014 Contest. For example, she made her Lemon-Blueberry Muffins out of Pillsbury Gluten Free refrigerated pie and pastry dough, repurposing a Pillsbury product in a traditional recipe. But unlike the German Chocolate Doughnuts, the muffins weren't Ode's favorite entry. "I was a little disappointed" that they were chosen over her other entries, she says. "I just didn't think it was the type of recipe that could actually win the Contest."

Will Ode try again? Now that her blog has generated income, General Mills may consider her a baking professional, in which case she wouldn't be permitted to compete unless the rules changed. "To tell you the truth, what I would really love to do is attend as media, as a blogger, to cover the event," she says. For anyone who does want to enter recipes, Ode has this advice: "Just try to come up with something that's original and different and maybe something that's trendy and just really delicious and easy." One person who may take that advice is her mother, who accompanied Ode to the 2013 Contest and was an early influence on her daughter's passion for baking. "She encouraged me to have a hobby and to be creative in the kitchen," says Ode. "She taught me how to measure properly, follow a recipe, and how to get creative by adding or substituting ingredients in an existing recipe to make it your own."

To stay creative with recipes, Ode likes to read magazines such as *Martha Stewart Living* and *Taste of Home* as well as cookbooks. But she doesn't get to watch many cooking shows on TV anymore. "I used to watch them a lot, but with the recipe creation on my blog, I really don't have time now," she says. Ode updates Mom Loves Baking often, which means she's continually developing recipes and designing the blog posts in a perfect marriage of her creative sensibilities. "I've always enjoyed art and baking," she says.

Sindee Morgan
Windsor, California

CONTEST 45 *Southwestern Corn Poppers*
CONTEST 47 *Navajo Chicken Tostadas*

Sindee Morgan's Pillsbury Bake-Off Contest experience began well before she ever entered a recipe. When she and her six younger sisters were growing up on a sheep farm in Sanpete County, Utah, they played "Pillsbury Bake-Off," making mud pies and sand pies to stand in for desserts. The girls would take turns being the judges, and as in the real Contest, they'd select a winning dish. "We would pretend to eat it, of course," says Morgan. "So I kind of had that little seed planted, but I didn't think I personally would ever have a chance [of getting into the Contest]. I always thought the Pillsbury Bake-Off winner was the best cook in the country. That was way beyond me."

A trip to New Zealand sparked an interest in reinvented recipes when Morgan met a cookbook writer who simplified the country's traditional dishes. And then, in the early 2000s, she saw the Pillsbury Bake-Off Contest on TV. "That's when it hit me that it was for the average American cook," she says. "I thought, You know, I think I could give that a try."

Morgan began entering the Contest in 2008, and in 2012 one of the five recipes she'd submitted was chosen: her Southwestern Corn Poppers, which she literally dreamed up. "I had been eating and drinking and sleeping Pillsbury Bake-Off, just trying to think of recipes, and I woke up having dreamed up a little recipe," she recalls. "I could see myself in my dream chopping up red bell peppers and corn, and I thought, Red bell peppers and corn go well together. Maybe I'll just start with that." To the peppers and corn she added green chiles, pepper Jack cheese, cream cheese, green onions, lime juice, and basil, and she baked the mixture in little cups made from Pillsbury Crescent rounds. By then, Morgan had been living in California for more than 20 years, and she says the fresh produce in her area had influenced the poppers recipe and her cooking in general.

Morgan's five children, all still living at home at the time, gave the poppers their approval, as did her husband and their neighbors. The day the Bake-Off team notified her that the recipe had been selected, "I couldn't quit smiling," she says. "It was truly one of the best days ever. It was just so exciting." But she couldn't tell other people just yet; General Mills instructs finalists to stay mum until it announces all the finalists and their recipes. "I felt like I was just bursting, because I wanted to tell everybody," she says.

At the competition, Morgan enjoyed meeting fellow home cooks from all over the United States. Throughout the event she thought of her grandmother, a prolific baker who sometimes made 15 small pies in a single day. "I kept thinking that she would be so excited to know that I had been able to go to the Pillsbury Bake-Off," Morgan says. Nicknamed the Cookie Lady, her grandmother "always had lots of cookies for the kids who would stop by on the way home from school" in Sanpete County, which Morgan describes as "a little farming community with lots of coal miners [that's] kind of a poor area." Morgan spent a lot of time learning how to cook at her grandmother's house, just a couple of miles from her childhood home. To this day, Morgan says, she cooks the "simple" kind of food she grew up with, such as homemade soups, and bakes her own bread.

Her memory of one dish from her childhood inspired her second Bake-Off finalist recipe, in Contest 47. "We had a lot of what they called Navajo Tacos, which is really a piece of fried bread, and then you pile all the makings of tacos on top," Morgan says. "I just kind of took what I had grown up with and made it a little simpler." She replaced some ingredients with roasted garlic Alfredo pasta sauce and used precooked chicken; for the fried bread, she cooked Pillsbury refrigerated biscuits in canola oil. The result: Navajo Chicken Tostadas, one of 20 recipes she entered in 2014.

Morgan advises Bake-Off hopefuls to explore their own food memories. "It helps to start with a recipe or two that you really like and then just simplify it," she says. "And think of ways that you can use Pillsbury products to substitute." When an idea occurs to her, she writes it in a notebook she keeps in the kitchen. "I have quite a list of ideas—just ideas—and then once the qualifying ingredients come out, I'll go through it and see if any of them fit the profile," says Morgan, who watches a number of shows on the Food Network as well as *MasterChef*. "Thinking of recipes is something I enjoy very much. Sometimes I find myself riding in the car and just occupying my time with thinking of recipes." Small wonder that she's planning a career in food: Once Morgan completes her certification as a registered dietary technician, she'll work alongside dietitians and nutritionists to write menus for people in varied settings.

Competing in the Bake-Off Contest has given Morgan the confidence of knowing that "it's possible to do some of these things that seemed like they were for other people," she says. She even uses the experience to give her children encouragement. When her daughter was having difficulty deciding whether to go back to school with two children at home, Morgan knew just what to do: "I wrote her a little note and said, 'If a little farm girl from Sanpete County, Utah, can make the Pillsbury Bake-Off, you can definitely go to school with two kids at home.'"

See also Marie Sheppard (page 10), Marie Valdes (page 33), Victoria Croce (page 37), Shana Butler (page 42), and Michele Kusma (page 47). Grand-prize winners Christina Verrelli (page 131) and Anna Ginsberg (page 135) have competed twice but are ineligible to participate in a future Bake-Off Contest, according to current rules.

CHAPTER 6

A First Taste of the Bake-Off Contest

ALL IT TAKES to become a lifelong fan of the Pillsbury Bake-Off Contest is to compete once. Lesley Pew, Kim Rollings, and Becky Pifer share their experiences as first-time finalists.

Lesley Pew
Lynn, Massachusetts

CONTEST 46 *Coconut Pecan Chocolate Fudge*

Lesley Pew has proved that sometimes the way into a baking contest is hiding in plain sight.

When the 46th Pillsbury Bake-Off Contest opened in 2013, Pew reviewed the list of eligible ingredients and saw that it included Pillsbury frosting in various flavors. Unfamiliar with the product, she went to the Pillsbury website (pillsbury.com) and searched for recipes made with frosting. "I found about 20 kinds of fudge," she says, "and I'm like, Oh, I didn't know you could make fudge with frosting." Pew, who says she had been trying to become a finalist for "many years," was intrigued. She knew that homemade fudge was made with butter, which helped the fudge harden in the refrigerator. But canned frosting contains oil instead of butter, so how did Pillsbury's fudge-from-frosting harden? After carefully reading the recipes, Pew realized they all called for melted baking chips—chocolate, vanilla, butterscotch, or peanut butter.

She took note of the combinations: Buttered Rum Fudge was made with vanilla frosting and butterscotch chips; Simple Peanut Butter Fudge contained chocolate-fudge frosting and peanut butter chips. She was especially interested in the layered fudge, which reminded her of the two-toned types she'd seen in candy shops. For example, Pillsbury's Double-Layer Mint Fudge has a bottom layer made with chocolate frosting and chocolate chips, and a top layer made with vanilla frosting and vanilla chips, flavored with crushed peppermint candy.

A FIRST TASTE OF THE BAKE-OFF CONTEST

"I was on a German chocolate cake kick" at the time, Pew says, so when she saw that one frosting flavor on the Bake-Off Contest's ingredient list was coconut pecan, her plan materialized. Pew created a bottom layer of fudge by combining chocolate frosting and chocolate chips, and a top layer from coconut pecan frosting and vanilla chips. To both layers she added pecans, coconut, and vanilla extract. "I used the same amount of chocolate chips and white chips" as in the pillsbury.com recipes, "because it looked like it had hardened up" the frosting sufficiently, she says. "When in doubt, follow the recipe." After winning enough online votes, her Coconut Pecan Chocolate Fudge made her a finalist in the Bake-Off Contest.

Pew describes her method as less than original ("I basically cloned somebody else's recipe"), but the fact is that Pillsbury encourages contestants to review the recipes on its website. And Pew made her entry stand apart from the pillsbury.com fudge recipes by putting her own twist on it, with a mash-up of German chocolate cake and fudge. "It was just different enough" to get into the Contest, "but it wasn't so far out there that nobody would touch it," she says.

Her goal was to become a finalist, though she says she "wouldn't mind" winning the grand prize. Over the years, Pew's husband and son have been her primary taste testers, but before she retired, she could also rely on her colleagues at the chain of community newspapers where she worked a combination of jobs—typesetter, interviewer, writer, layout artist. "The reporters would wolf down anything," she says. "I put things in the employees' kitchen thinking, Nobody will touch this, and I go in 15 minutes later and I'm like, Where did they put those cookies?" Her Crab Rangoon was especially popular. "I could barely get it in the door, and it would be gone," she says.

Pew, who describes herself as equally a cook and a baker, grew up watching Julia Child on TV and perusing the recipe magazines that Pillsbury published after each Bake-Off Contest. Today she reads food magazines, but "I wish *Gourmet* were still in existence," she says, adding that she frequently sees problems with the recipes she reads elsewhere. "Nobody knows their measurements. Three teaspoons equals a tablespoon. Why didn't you just write one tablespoon?" Another problem: "You'll have lemon zest in a recipe, and it will say 'lemon rind.' I don't want the rind; the rind is the entire thing. The white part is the pith, and the zest is the yellow part. You want the zest, not the rind," says Pew, who worked as a technical typesetter in a scientific lab earlier in her career.

Her precision has gotten her into a variety of contests, among them the Great Garlic Cook-Off and the IGA National Hometown Holidays Recipe Challenge. Since returning from the 46th Pillsbury Bake-Off Contest, "I'm getting more adventurous," she says. "I'm entering fewer contests, but I'm being more creative about which ones and what the recipes are, and I'm getting to go places." The Bake-Off Contest in which she competed was held in Las Vegas, where she "had been itching to go, but we never really had the money to do it," she says. Because General Mills paid for her airfare from Massachusetts as well as two nights in a hotel, she was able to see Vegas and tack on tours of the Grand Canyon and the Hoover Dam. But the best thing about the trip? "I got to meet a lot of people that I would never have met otherwise, and I'm still talking to some of them online," she says.

Finding herself a bit bored with retirement, Pew took a job in a supermarket in the summer of 2016. On one side of the store she smelled cakes and cookies baking, and on the other she took in savory aromas from rotisserie chickens and other dishes. No matter where she stood, she thought of recipes. Mindful of the one that got her into the 46th Pillsbury Bake-Off Contest, she encourages Bake-Off hopefuls to take the route she took. "Look on the website," she says. "It won't say explicitly, 'This is what we want,' but it's what they already have. It's a big company, and they have kitchens that test everything."

Kim Rollings
Dallas

CONTEST 44 *Muffuletta Quiche Cups*

A few weeks before Kim Rollings competed in the Bake-Off Contest, her local Kroger supermarket wished her well in a very public way: with a huge billboard that said GOOD LUCK KIM AT THE 44TH PILLSBURY BAKE-OFF CONTEST 2010! over her full name. "It stayed up for six months, so over the course of that time, everyone said, 'That's you!'" Rollings says with a laugh. And when those people asked whether she'd won, her response was, and still is, a very positive no. "I think just going was amazing," she says. "Winning would be great, but I wouldn't trade that experience for anything."

That experience got its start in 2001, the year after Rollings won the grand prize in a contest sponsored by the National Potato Promotion Board. Encouraged by the win, she began entering other contests, "and when the Bake-Off came up, I decided to give it a try," she says. "I didn't get chosen, but it was fun, and after that I had the bug." The fourth time she entered, in 2010, the Bake-Off team selected her Muffuletta Quiche Cups, inspired by the muffuletta sandwiches of New Orleans, where Rollings lived for a while. What sets a muffuletta apart from other hero-type sandwiches is its olive salad, which consists of a dozen ingredients. Rollings simplified it: "I used [pimiento-stuffed] green olives and oregano to kind of match that," she says. She then mixed the other filling ingredients together and divided them among eight cups she'd formed from Pillsbury Crescent rolls. "It's pretty tasty, but pressing the Crescent rolls into the muffin cups was a bit of a job," she says. "I can see why the recipe didn't win just from a preparation standpoint."

Rollings generally waits for the eligible ingredients to be announced before she begins thinking of Bake-Off recipes. Then she lets them "just roll around" in her mind, she says, a process that she considers both fun and challenging: "How can I possibly make something that nobody else has done and will wow the judges?" One recipe she admires is the grand-prize winner the year she competed, the Mini Ice Cream Cookie Cups, entered by Sue Compton of Delanco, New Jersey. "It was very creative, very simple, and so adaptable," she says. "Immediately I thought of all the ways she could have improvised on that. And it was so pretty." Some critics complained that the ice cream cups weren't so much baked or cooked as assembled, but Rollings sees that aspect as a benefit. "I think that appeals to the general public," she says. "A lot of people don't cook."

Rollings's taste testers over the years have included "my neighbors and my kids and my family and my office," she says. Sometimes her husband, Bill, would take her dishes to his office and place a sheet of paper next to them with a note. For a Welsh rarebit cheesecake starter she was testing, Bill wrote, "This is an original creation by Kim Rollings that will be entered in a cooking contest. It is an appetizer. Please take a bite and give her your opinion on the sheet below. She is an experienced cook who is not afraid of the 'TRUTH.'" At the end of the day, he'd hand the sheet to Rollings. The comments about the Welsh rarebit appetizers were typical: Along with multiple compliments were suggestions to add more spice. "I don't equate Welsh rarebit with spicy heat, but that's a Texas thing," says Rollings, who has lived in Dallas since the 1980s.

A precise person ("I'm a proofreader for a living, so that says it all"), Rollings has entered only one or two recipes per contest. "I want it to be perfect so it won't be eliminated for one of the wrong reasons," she says. The Muffuletta Quiche Cups were Rollings's only entry in the 44th Bake-Off Contest, and the news that they were chosen brightened a bad day. Just hours before Rollings got the call from General Mills, Bill had had surgery for prostate cancer. By the time the Bake-Off Contest was held, he felt well enough to accompany her. "He was so proud of me," she says. "The Bake-Off helped us all through that year." Bill died in 2013, but the memory of his presence at the Contest is "a special part of the Bake-Off," she says.

Since competing at the Contest, Rollings has been encouraging others to enter. "But I don't think anyone has," she says. "They go, 'Oh, I could never do that,' and I say, 'Sure! Just get a can of Crescent dough and play with it and see what comes to mind. I've come up with some real duds. Just keep on trying.' But people have other interests." And not everyone had both a mother and a mother-in-law who were excellent cooks, or took inspiration from cookbooks by Julia Child, Craig Claiborne, and Marcella Hazan. Today Rollings enjoys watching cooking shows featuring Ina Garten, Giada De Laurentiis, and Bobby Flay and reading magazines such as *Food & Wine* and *Saveur*. "There are too many. I'm trying to pare them down," she says. "But I just love them."

Although Rollings hasn't been a Bake-Off finalist since 2010, her coworkers continue to mention the Contest and ask whether she's entered it lately. "I guess that's my claim to fame," she says.

A FIRST TASTE OF THE BAKE-OFF CONTEST

"It still sticks in people's minds." And that, she says, is part of the appeal: "I think the celebrity of it was fun for me and for all my friends and colleagues, too. We just had a good time with it. I have a lot of pleasant memories and friendships, lots of good memories. It was a great part of my life experience."

Becky Pifer
Blanchard, Michigan

CONTEST 45 *Peanut Butter Crunch Layer Bars*

If ever anyone had the right to think it was easy to get into the Pillsbury Bake-Off Contest, it would have to be Becky Pifer in 2012. Pifer became a finalist with the first recipe she'd ever entered, and she hadn't even prepared it before submitting it. "I just kind of looked at the ingredient list, and just from my background in baking and throwing things together, I decided that was my recipe right then and there," she says of her Peanut Butter Crunch Layer Bars, made from Pillsbury refrigerated peanut butter cookie dough, chocolate chips, toffee bits, and other ingredients.

But Pifer knew better than to think it was easy, especially after connecting with other Bake-Off finalists on Facebook before the competition. "They were all talking about how many years they had been trying and how many recipes they had submitted," she says. "So I really just attributed it to a great deal of luck that first time."

Pifer had actually tested and submitted a second recipe, but she had spent so little time on the peanut butter bar entry that when General Mills called with questions about it, "I truly couldn't remember what it was," she says. Once the caller refreshed her memory, she understood the appeal. "The flavors are so universal. Everyone loves peanut butter and chocolate together," Pifer says. "And it's so easy to make—it literally is just throwing some things in a bowl. You can teach your children how to bake with it."

After enjoying every aspect of the 45th Pillsbury Bake-Off Contest, right down to submitting her dish to the judges, she started thinking of recipes that would bring her back. "Sometimes I'll have ideas while I'm on the road," says Pifer, a software trainer who travels often for work and inquires about local dishes wherever she goes. Occasionally she's inspired when she's grocery shopping and sees a new product from Pillsbury or a previous Contest cosponsor. "I'll pick up new ingredients and try to come up with something new and fun and have people try it," even before she knows what the eligible products for the next Contest will be, she says.

Sometimes ideas creep into Pifer's mind when she's relaxed—for instance, on her morning walk or even in a dream. Other times they may be prompted by a story in one of the many food magazines she reads in airports. "If I'm reading an article, I'll just jot down some general ideas: 'Oh, I think that would be a good recipe for submission,' and I'll play with it after," says Pifer, whose culinary hobby was inspired by both her mother, a Southern cook, and her stepmother, a caterer who often created shortcuts when preparing food.

A baker since childhood, Pifer says her taste testers include her husband, daughter, and son-in-law, as well as other relatives, but she has an even bigger test market: the 90 young women in the sorority she advises at Central Michigan University. "I bake for them quite often," she says, "and I'll get their opinions about what they like and don't like." Pifer doesn't always have to ask for their feedback; if a dish has been devoured quickly, she knows it has potential. "That's kind of the one I'll lean toward and maybe tweak a little," she says.

Pifer entered Bake-Off Contests 46 and 47 with five taste-tested recipes in each, some savory and some sweet. She didn't make it in, and she has since decided to remove savory submissions from her Bake-Off repertoire. "My favorites are always the sweet things, and I think that's probably where I will focus from now on," she says. She'll also try to keep her recipes up-to-date and easy: "In my opinion, the Bake-Off, at least recently, has been looking for trends and ways to do things very simply, so that's kind of where my mind runs when I'm thinking about potential entries."

One way Pifer keeps up with the culinary world is by watching *The Kitchen* on the Food Network. "They do a lot of fun and trendy things, shortcuts and things like that, that I'm always looking for," she says. "I don't have a lot of spare time. I'm trying to find things that I can make quickly that both my family and friends will enjoy." Pifer's job limits the time she spends on her hobby, but they have one thing in common. "Creativity is a big factor in both Bake-Off recipes and my job," she says. "I have to continually be creative helping clients to build reports that are maybe not traditionally what they're thinking of."

When she returned from the 45th Bake-Off Contest, Pifer says, she felt "a little more confident" in herself as a baking contestant, so she entered the local Shepherd Maple Syrup Festival competition—and won. "At this point, having been away from [the Bake-Off Contest] since 2012, I think I'm back to my old self: still baking, still confident in what I bake, but if it's award winning I'm happy, and if it's not, I'm still happy," says Pifer. Yet one thing hasn't changed. "I'm still obsessed with the Doughboy," she says. "Any time I see a Doughboy, it makes me smile."

See also Heidi Givler, page 18; Marie Bruno, page 22; Carole Resnick, page 51; and Linda Drumm, page 60.

CHAPTER 7

Winners' Circle

FROM 1996, when Pillsbury increased the grand prize to seven figures, to 2014, the most recent Contest year as of this writing, 11 Bake-Off finalists were each awarded $1 million. Three of those winners are Beth Royals, Christina Verrelli, and Anna Ginsberg, who discuss here how they won the most competitive cooking contest in the United States.

All the grand-prize winners—whether they were awarded $25,000 in 1949 or $50,000 in 1995 or $1 million in 2014—demonstrated an ability to think creatively with food, to come up with a unique idea, and to follow through on it with a practical recipe. Since 1966, grand-prize winners have been ineligible to enter future Bake-Off Contests.

Beth Royals
Richmond, Virginia

CONTEST 41 **Shrimp Salad Pita-Wiches**
CONTEST 42 **Vermont Maple Bread Pudding**
CONTEST 47 **Peanutty Pie Crust Clusters** GRAND-PRIZE WINNER

Some recipes in the Pillsbury Bake-Off Contest are the result of careful planning, meant to fulfill a particular purpose. Others are more spontaneous, coming together in a single inspired moment. Beth Royals's grand-prize-winning recipe, Peanutty Pie Crust Clusters, was both.

When the 47th Bake-Off Contest started accepting recipes in February 2014, Royals had a plan. "My goal was to use pie crust in a way that hadn't been done before," she says. "I wanted to come up with a creative way to put it inside something," since most contestants either used it as a whole crust or wrapped it around a filling. "I started to think, I can't heat it inside something; it's just not going to cook. I'm going to have to break it down into smaller parts." So she cut the crust into tiny squares and baked them. What to do with the baked squares? She tried putting them in parfaits, but they became soggy. She tried adding them to cobbler toppings, but they lost their crispness there, too. And then inspiration struck.

"I happened to be making drop candies, and it was just one of those moments that clicked," says Royals, who had been in the habit of combining leftover chocolate with nuts, fruit, and chopped pretzels. Realizing the pie crust squares would stay crisp in a drop candy, the way chow mein noodles do in chocolate haystacks, she chose her ingredients. "I tried to incorporate a variety of textures: flaky pie crust, crunchy toffee, and melty vanilla chips," she says. For a second eligible product (the first was the Pillsbury refrigerated pie crust), she used Crisco Baking Sticks Butter Flavor All-Vegetable Shortening. Jif Peanut Butter was also eligible, but Royals used only a tablespoonful—not enough to qualify, yet "I felt I was still getting a lot of products in there that were part of the General Mills family," she says.

At the same time, Royals tried not to use so many ingredients that the recipe became fussy or complicated. Contestants in the 47th Bake-Off competition were limited to seven ingredients per recipe, but Royals drew the line at six. "I was going to drizzle [the clusters] with maybe a different-color chocolate on top, and I said, You know what, I'm just going to try to keep this as quick and easy and streamlined as I can," she says.

Her decision paid off. The Peanutty Pie Crust Clusters won the sweets category at the 47th Bake-Off Contest, at which point General Mills put it up for an internet vote against the three other category winners for the grand prize: Creamy Corn–Filled Sweet Peppers, Cuban-Style Sandwich Pockets, and Chocolate Doughnut Poppers. Of the four recipes, Royals's was the only one that had put a Pillsbury product inside a dish, as opposed to wrapping it around something (for example, the Chocolate Doughnut Poppers wrapped Pillsbury Crescent dough around Jif Chocolate Hazelnut Spread). A month later, on the ABC-TV show *The Chew*, Royals was named the million-dollar winner.

"We thought Beth's idea, to use Pillsbury refrigerated pie crust in a candy-like recipe, was both unique and creative," Jann Atkins, the Bake-Off Contest's kitchen manager, said at the time. "This dish is easy to make, and it stores very well, making it a great contribution to holiday parties and potlucks." (See recipe, page 156.)

Photos of the clusters quickly started showing up on social media, occasionally with variations: Some people sprinkled them with red and green nonpareils for the holidays; Lise Sullivan Ode, another Contest 47 finalist and the blogger behind Mom Loves Baking (see page 104), made a semisweet chocolate version. A columnist for the *Houston Chronicle* decided to ditch the recipes she had planned to publish and gave her readers the cluster recipe instead. "They looked so good, I had to try them out," the columnist, Elizabeth Pudwill, wrote. "The combination of flaky bits of pie crust, salty peanuts and sweet melty white chocolate with peanut butter is awesome."

The clusters were Royals's third finalist recipe; she had competed with her Shrimp Salad Pita-Wiches in 2004 and her Vermont Maple Bread Pudding in 2006. Royals started entering the Pillsbury Bake-Off Contest in 2002, after winning other competitions. First was *Nick Jr.* magazine's Cooking With Kids contest, which awarded Royals and her son, then four years old, the grand prize for their healthful birthday-cake-style pancake recipe. Shortly thereafter, she won the grand prize in the Great Garlic Cook-Off, where another finalist clued her in to the active world of cooking contests. "She kind of opened my eyes to what was out there," says Royals, whose contest honors now include many grand prizes and first-place wins from companies such as Baker's and Quaker Oats.

But she tried not to think of other companies whenever she entered the Pillsbury Bake-Off Contest, to separate it in her mind from competitions that sought more gourmet or complicated recipes. "I had to get into the mode of thinking convenience and shorter titles, catchy titles," Royals says. "It really was just a whole different way that I went about that contest." She'd make a list of the recipes she wanted to test, covering all the categories and as many product groups as possible, "in case they're looking to fill a spot," she says—for example, if the Bake-Off team needed another Pillsbury Crescent dough recipe to round out the 100. For the dinner category, she'd try to have a chicken, a beef, and a pork recipe, "just realizing that there's a thought process on their end. If they've already got the top ones and they're all chicken, they're probably going to try to find a beef one," she says.

Royals entered a total of eight Pillsbury Bake-Off Contests and submitted an average of 10 recipes in each. That includes some dishes she wasn't wild about. "When in doubt, send it out," she says. "I won a grand prize once in a contest where the particular flavor combination didn't appeal to me, but I sent it in anyway."

Much as Royals enjoys strategizing with recipes, the real motivation behind her cooking-contest hobby has been the friendships she's formed. "It's just a great support system, and [the other contestants] all have the same passion and desire to cook and bake for other people," she says. "It gives them joy, and I automatically click with those personalities. I kept wanting to get back together and see people." Her two sons have occasionally joined in the adventures: One accompanied her on a contest trip to Disney World, and the other went with her to New York City. "There's just been fun times and fun memories that our family has experienced through it," she says.

Royals and her husband have used some of the Bake-Off winnings—which come in 20 annual installments of $50,000, before taxes—to make repairs on their house and help others in their community, and a chunk of it will pay for the boys' college education. "People ask me why I'm still working," says Royals, a sales representative for a marketing company. "In today's times, for me, it's important and necessary." People have also asked her whether she's taken extravagant vacations or bought a new car. "We're pretty much the same as we were before," she says. "No real splurges. We're just being smart about it."

Her Bake-Off win was a long time coming. Royals has been cooking and baking from a young age, taught by her father, Henry Hirschy, a Navy man who was the director of executive dining facilities at the White House during the Kennedy administration. "He was adventurous in the kitchen and always kept detailed notes in his collection of cookbooks of variations he tried on recipes," she says. "He introduced me to a variety of ethnic cuisines, unique ingredients, and flavor combinations I would never have tried if it weren't for him." Their time together in the kitchen gave her a sense of accomplishment and left her with happy memories of cooking with Hirschy, who died four months after she won the Pillsbury Bake-Off Contest. It also taught her a life lesson: "I quickly made the association that cooking and baking were great ways to give of myself and show my love for others," she says.

Royals's cooking-contest hobby lets her put that lesson into practice. She often freezes her creations so that she'll have them on hand to share with others—maybe someone at her church who has a need, maybe the school bus driver. "There's always somebody whose mood can be lifted through food," she says.

WINNERS' CIRCLE

Christina Verrelli
Devon, Pennsylvania

CONTEST 44 *Savory and Sweet Breakfast Biscuit Sliders*
CONTEST 45 *Pumpkin Ravioli With Salted Caramel Whipped Cream* GRAND-PRIZE WINNER

Christina Verrelli decided to enter only two kinds of recipes in the 2012 Pillsbury Bake-Off Contest: desserts and chicken dishes. "If you look through the years, there were a lot of dessert winners and a lot of chicken winners," she says. Her strategy worked: Verrelli's Pumpkin Ravioli With Salted Caramel Whipped Cream, a dessert, won the million-dollar grand prize.

It was no off-the-cuff recipe. "I worked on that one for a good week," she says about the dish, which calls for filling Pillsbury Crescent dough squares with a spiced mixture of pumpkin and cream cheese. "I had to figure out just the right texture so that [the filling] wouldn't squeeze out when you formed the ravioli. I went back and forth to the grocery store quite a bit." Of the seven recipes she submitted that year, the pumpkin ravioli was among her favorites, and she was happy to learn it had been chosen for competition. But she doubted it would win a prize, for two reasons: First, pumpkin is generally considered a fall ingredient, and the 2012 Bake-Off Contest took place in the spring. Second, the recipe "was a little more complicated to make than some of the other winners," she says. "I didn't have a good feeling about it."

But the Bake-Off judges did. After the competition, one of them, Carolyn Jung, wrote on her blog, FoodGal (foodgal.com), "Round and round it went, until we finally came to unanimity on the dish that really merited the top prize: 'Pumpkin Ravioli With Salted Caramel Whipped Cream.'

"Why? Because when you took one bite, you wanted to devour the entire thing. Fresh out of the oven, the hand pie–like 'raviolis' were crisp, puffy and covered in cinnamon sugar like wonderful beignets that take far more effort to make. The pumpkin–cream cheese filling was fluffy and redolent of vanilla and autumn spices. It was a recipe that felt modern and timely. And it would no doubt appeal to kids and adults alike."

When Martha Stewart announced on her TV show that Verrelli had won the dessert category, Verrelli popped up from her seat in the audience excitedly, scarcely believing the news. And when Stewart announced that Verrelli had won the grand prize, there were happy tears, hearty cheers, and a whole lot of confetti.

Verrelli had been a finalist once before, the only other time she'd entered the Pillsbury Bake-Off Contest—in 2010, with her Savory and Sweet Breakfast Biscuit Sliders. At the time, she'd never entered a cooking competition, but after seeing an ad for the Bake-Off Contest in a magazine, she went to pillsbury.com and read the rules. "I just figured, I've got nothing to lose. I'll make something and make it for my family for dinner," she says. "I really didn't think I would get in. I kind of entered on a whim." Once she had created three dishes, she gave her husband and two daughters portions for taste testing, along with scorecards so they could record their impressions. "I wanted to see if they were worthy of sending in," Verrelli says of her first original recipes.

She was already somewhat familiar with the competition because her mother had bought a couple of the Pillsbury Bake-Off Contest's recipe magazines when Verrelli was a child. Cooking since the age of seven, Verrelli, the youngest of six children, learned at her mother's side, both in the kitchen and at the grocery store. She's been watching PBS cooking shows since she was a teenager, and today she also reads magazines such as *Cook's Illustrated, Better Homes and Gardens,* and *Cuisine at Home.*

A former elementary-school teacher, Verrelli took 11 years off to raise her daughters and was just getting back into teaching when she won the Bake-Off Contest. As her attention shifted to the culinary world, she started a blog, Epicuricloud (epicuricloud.com), where she explains and illustrates recipes. It also features a section called "10 Winning Tips for the Pillsbury Bake-Off Contest," which discusses everything from doing your Contest homework to planning your game-day strategy.

In 2014, Verrelli was chosen to compete on the Food Network show *America's Best Cook,* where she impressed the judges with her skills and her grace under pressure. "That was one crazy experience," says Verrelli, who finished as the runner-up. "It was just so outside my comfort zone." After shooting for 18 hours at a time and worrying about what cooking surprise she'd encounter next, she isn't sure she'd do it again. "But it was a lot of fun, and it was probably good training for what I do now," Verrelli says. What she does now is represent KitchenAid on QVC, developing recipes and demonstrating them using the brand's appliances and related products.

The Bake-Off Contest "helped open all these doors to a new career for me," says Verrelli. "I never would have gotten this job if I hadn't done that. I don't think I would have done the Food Network show if I hadn't done that." It's also possible that she wouldn't have entered other contests, such as National Beef Cook-Off and the World Food Championships, as she did for a few years after her first Pillsbury turn.

These days Verrelli doesn't have the time it takes to enter contests. "I would say that all the creativity and fun that I had creating recipes for contests I now do for the blog and for my demonstrations on TV for KitchenAid," she says. Happy as she is in her new career, she says it isn't even the best thing that came out of competing in the Pillsbury Bake-Off Contest. "Hands down, [it was] getting to meet the people," she says, especially those she continues to correspond with online. "We enjoyed our time with one another. It's neat how you can meet people who have the same interests as you, but they're all different ages, from all different parts of the country, and you come together with this common interest of food and being creative with food."

WINNERS' CIRCLE

Anna Ginsberg
Chicago

CONTEST 41 *Spicy Barbecue Triangles With Raita*
CONTEST 42 *Baked Chicken and Spinach Stuffing* GRAND-PRIZE WINNER

Oprah Winfrey was impressed. There she was, watching Anna Ginsberg demonstrate her grand-prize-winning recipe on the set of *The Oprah Winfrey Show,* when Ginsberg started to sauté cubed waffle sticks with a chopped onion to make stuffing. "I never would have thought of this in my whole life, to put waffle sticks with onions," Winfrey said. "I see why you won, girl!"

Ginsberg's Baked Chicken and Spinach Stuffing, the winning recipe in the 2006 Pillsbury Bake-Off Contest, may sound pedestrian, but it was off the charts in originality. One of her eligible products was Pillsbury Dunkables frozen waffle sticks, which came with packets of maple syrup. Ginsberg created stuffing by mixing the waffle sticks, an onion, chicken broth, poultry seasoning, and other ingredients, to which she added Green Giant frozen spinach, her second eligible product. The rules required her to use the maple syrup, too, so she combined it with peach preserves and Worcestershire sauce to make a sweet glaze, which she spread on two chicken breasts before baking them.

"It's not a lot of work but feels restauranty in the good sense of the word," one of the judges, Martha Holmberg, told the *American-Statesman* of Austin, Texas, where Ginsberg was living at the time. "The waffle fingers had a nice texture and it was a good way to get spinach and vegetables in there. It's a complete dinner."

Ginsberg told Winfrey the recipe had come to her "in a flash," but today she has a different idea of what that means. "Everything seems to come in a flash," Ginsberg says. "But I think in reality, ideas incubate for a while, and your brain is influenced by things around you. Maybe I had chicken and waffles on the brain. Maybe I had been craving stuffing." She already had experience making chicken dishes with sweet sauces. "So it seemed like it came together in a flash, but it probably didn't," says Ginsberg. After the idea occurred to her, she made the recipe quickly and liked the results. "I made it again, and it all worked out," she says. (The Dunkables waffle sticks have since been discontinued.)

The chicken dish was Ginsberg's second finalist recipe, and the 2006 Bake-Off Contest was the fourth one she'd entered. She'd gotten into the 2004 Contest with a recipe that didn't win a prize but stood out nonetheless: Spicy Barbecue Triangles With Raita, Indian pastries she'd made from chicken in barbecue sauce, cumin, cayenne, and the Indian spice blend garam masala, all wrapped in Pillsbury Crescent dinner rolls. For the raita, a condiment that counterbalances spicy flavors, she mixed yogurt and a chopped cucumber.

Ginsberg entered about 50 recipes in each Bake-Off Contest. "I was kind of a recipe-creating maniac back then," she says. "It's like a puzzle. You try to find the products that nobody else is using, or the products that you think they want to highlight, and make it different, because that's the whole goal: You've got to do something that nobody else has done. So I would just come up with all kinds of ideas, and I submitted every one to the Bake-Off."

She's not an advocate of the perfect-just-one-recipe school of thought: "That's good if your recipe is great and you really know what you're doing. But sometimes it's good to come up with a bunch of smaller ideas, execute them, and submit them. With the Bake-Off, I think that's the best strategy. They're going to change it a bit anyway. They really want your idea and your originality."

Ginsberg was so prolific in those days that she not only developed scores of recipes for the Pillsbury Bake-Off Contest but also baked a batch of cookies every day, often giving them to friends and neighbors. In 2005 she started a blog, Cookie Madness (cookiemadness.net), which initially provided recipes just for cookies and other sweets. Today the blog is so comprehensive that the categories number in the 200s and extend into crackers, yeast breads, pizza dough, pancakes, and biscuits.

Since winning the Bake-Off Contest, Ginsberg has written a book, *The Daily Cookie: 365 Tempting Treats for the Sweetest Year of Your Life* (Andrews McMeel), which gives a cookie recipe for each of the historical and pop-culture events that are commemorated in a year. What to make for Elvis Presley's birthday? Peanut Browned Butter Banana-Bacon Cookies. For Squirrel Appreciation Day? Caramel Nut Bars. With a five-star rating on amazon.com, the book has reviews that include customer comments like "Clear instructions, beautiful pictures and a huge variety" and "I first found this book at the library and omg I loved it that much I had to buy it."

Is there another book in her future? "I would love to write one, but there are so many cookbooks out there right now, I don't know what I would write about," Ginsberg says. "It seems like everything's been done." Much as she likes cookbooks, she doesn't buy many anymore. "I do most of my recipe shopping online now," she says. "I'll buy a book only if it's by a chef that I really like at a restaurant or somebody who has a lot of tips that I'm going to learn something from." One author whose cookbooks Ginsberg buys is Robin Miller, known for her five-ingredient recipes. "Inevitably you're going to add more [ingredients], but she gives you the basics, and you might never have thought these things could go well together," says Ginsberg. She also buys books of vegan and gluten-free recipes, "because that's all new to me," she explains.

Although she used to watch *Top Chef*, she isn't a fan of cooking shows on TV, especially the competitive ones. "Watching people on TV compete against each other just gets me riled up," says Ginsberg, adding that she hasn't watched the Food Network "in ages." But she does read *Food Network Magazine*. "It's kind of fun and soothing to look at," she says. "Maybe I'm just more of a reader." Other magazines she reads include *Family Circle* ("They have a really good food editor; they always have new things"), *Real Simple* ("It always has good ideas"), *Food & Wine*, *Cooking Light*, and *EatingWell*.

Ginsberg didn't grow up with food magazines or cookbooks. "My mom didn't cook at all," she says. So Ginsberg taught herself how to bake and cook, starting at age six, when she was a latchkey kid. "I had a lot of time by myself, so I would play in the kitchen," she says. She remembers being "obsessed" with baking sugar cookies—"I wanted to use cookie cutters"—and learning how to make them from a *Sesame Street* book that featured Cookie Monster and Big Bird. The cookies turned out well, but she had less success with a soufflé, which she made from a recipe for adults. "I wanted to surprise my mom with a cheese soufflé, and I didn't know cooking terms because I was so young, but I followed the directions in a rudimentary way," she says. The baked soufflé was only an inch high. "It was more like a quiche," Ginsberg says. "My mom came home and ate it. She was so happy, just because she had something. It was probably my first big disaster, and I've had several since."

But her disasters are far outnumbered by her contest wins. In fact, Ginsberg won the first baking contest she'd ever entered, a Kraft competition, with her chocolate-hazelnut cheesecake. She followed that up with awards and honors from California Raisins, Betty Crocker, and others.

About seven years after winning the Pillsbury Bake-Off Contest, Ginsberg became the food editor of *Texas Co-op Power* magazine, which goes out to members of an electric cooperative that serves many small, rural areas in the Lone Star State. The food section consists of reader recipes, and every month the magazine sponsors a contest. "My job was helping to select the recipes," Ginsberg says. "We'd all bake or cook them and then rate them. There would be a winner every month. It was the greatest job ever. I loved it so much."

Unfortunately, she had to give up the position when she moved to Illinois in 2015. "My boss needed the person to be local," Ginsberg says. She'd like to find something similar in Chicago, though she's been busy with volunteer work for two organizations that host dinners for the homeless. For one she bakes, and for the other she helps serve food and clean up. And she continues to update her blog, adding a new post every couple of days.

Just past the midway point in her 20 years of annual payouts for her Bake-Off prize, Ginsberg says winning the Pillsbury Bake-Off Contest has "taken away a lot of financial burdens or worries." She and her husband used some of the earliest payments to remodel their kitchen, and they've been setting aside money to cover college tuition for their daughter. She was only four years old when Ginsberg won the Bake-Off Contest, and now she's starting to think about a college major.

In that decade, Ginsberg has maintained the friendships she formed at the Bake-Off Contest. "I think Pillsbury attracts a lot of creative people," she says. "All the people who were there were kind of fun—just nice people, good people. So, for me, I think making friends was probably one of the best things about it. I don't like everybody, but I like Bake-Off people."

APPENDIX A

Pillsbury Bake-Off Contest Winners

#	YEAR	RECIPE	WINNER	PILLSBURY PRODUCT
1	1949	No-Knead Water-Rising Twists	Theodora Smafield	Flour
2	1950	Orange Kiss-Me Cake	Lily Wuebel	Flour
3	1951	Starlight Double-Delight Cake	Helen Weston	Flour
4	1952	Snappy Turtle Cookies	Beatrice Harlib	Flour
5	1953	"My Inspiration" Cake	Lois Kanago	Flour
6	1954	Open Sesame Pie	Dorothy Koteen	Flour
7	1955	Ring-a-Lings	Bertha Jorgensen	Flour
8	1956	California Casserole	Hildreth Hatheway	Flour
9	1957	Accordion Treats	Gerda Roderer	Flour
10	1958	Spicy Apple Twists	Dorothy DeVault	Flour
11	1959	Mardi Gras Party Cake	Eunice G. Surles	Flour
12	1960	Dilly Casserole Bread	Leona Schnuelle	Flour
13	1961	Candy Bar Cookies	Alice Reese	Flour
14	1962	Apple Pie '63	Julia Smogor	Flour
15	1963	Hungry Boys' Casserole	Mira Walilko	Flour
16	1964	Peacheesy Pie	Janis Boykin	Flour
17	1966	Golden Gate Snack Bread	Mari Petrelli	Flour
18	1967	Muffin Mix Buffet Bread	Maxine Bullock	Flour

PILLSBURY BAKE-OFF CONTEST WINNERS

#	YEAR	RECIPE	WINNER	PILLSBURY PRODUCT
19	1968	Buttercream Pound Cake	Phyllis Lidert	Flour
20	1969	Magic Marshmallow Crescent Puffs	Edna Walker	Crescent dinner rolls
21	1970	Onion Lover's Twist	Nan Robb	Flour
22	1971	Pecan Pie Surprise Bars	Pearl Hall	Cake mix
23	1972*	Streusel Spice Cake	Rose DeDominicis	Cake mix
		Quick and Chewy Crescent Bars	Isabelle Collins	Crescent dinner rolls, flour
24	1973	Quick Crescent Pecan Pie Bars	Albina Flieller	Crescent dinner rolls
		Banana Crunch Cake	Bonnie Brooks	Cake mix, flour
25	1974	Chocolate Cherry Bars	Francis I. Jerzak	Cake mix
		Savory Crescent Chicken Squares	Doris Castle	Crescent dinner rolls
26	1975	Easy Crescent Danish Rolls	Barbara S. Gibson	Crescent dinner rolls
		Sour Cream Apple Squares	Luella Maki	Flour
27	1976	Crescent Caramel Swirl	Lois Ann Groves	Crescent dinner rolls
		Whole Wheat Raisin Loaf	Lenora H. Smith	Flour
28	1978	Nutty Graham Picnic Cake	Esther Tomich	Flour
		Chick-n-Broccoli Pot Pies	Linda Wood	Biscuits
29	1980	Italian Zucchini Crescent Pie	Millicent (Caplan) Nathan	Crescent dinner rolls
30	1982	Almond-Filled Cookie Cake	Elizabeth Meijer	Flour
31	1984	Country Apple Coffee Cake	Susan Porubcan	Biscuits
32	1986	Apple Nut Lattice Tart	Mary Lou Warren	Pie crust
33	1988	Chocolate Praline Layer Cake	Julie Bengtson	Cake mix
34	1990	Blueberry–Poppy Seed Brunch Cake	Linda Rahman	Flour
35	1992	Pennsylvania Dutch Cake and Custard Pie	Gladys Fulton	Pie crust
36	1994	Fudgy Bonbons	Mary Anne Tyndall	Flour
37	1996	Macadamia Fudge Torte	Kurt Wait	Cake mix

PILLSBURY BAKE-OFF CONTEST WINNERS

#	YEAR	RECIPE	WINNER	PILLSBURY PRODUCT
38	1998	Salsa Couscous Chicken	Ellie Mathews	No Pillsbury product†
39	2000	Cream Cheese Brownie Pie	Roberta Sonefeld	Pie crust, brownie mix
40	2002	Chicken Florentine Panini	Denise JoAnne Yennie	Pizza crust
41	2004	Oats and Honey Granola Pie	Suzanne Conrad	Pie crust
42	2006	Baked Chicken and Spinach Stuffing	Anna Ginsberg	Pillsbury Dunkables frozen waffle sticks
43	2008	Double-Delight Peanut Butter Cookies	Carolyn Gurtz	Cookie dough
44	2010	Mini Ice Cream Cookie Cups	Sue Compton	Cookie dough
45	2012	Pumpkin Ravioli With Salted Caramel Whipped Cream	Christina Verrelli	Crescent Dough Sheet, flour
46	2013	Loaded Potato Pinwheels	Glori Spriggs	Crescent Dough Sheet or dinner rolls
47	2014	Peanutty Pie Crust Clusters	Beth Royals	Pie crust

*From 1972 to 1978, each Pillsbury Bake-Off Contest had two grand-prize winners.

†No Pillsbury product was required in 1998. The winning recipe contained Old El Paso salsa, owned then by Pillsbury and now by General Mills.

APPENDIX B

Bake-Off Recipes That Repurposed Pillsbury Products

Many of the finalists interviewed for *Smart Cookies* said they thought their recipes had made it into the Pillsbury Bake-Off Contest because they'd used an eligible product in a creative way. Kellie White (see page 95) said her two finalist recipes, which both won awards, "did something different with the Pillsbury ingredients that hadn't been done before, and I think [the judges] like that."

Here's a sampling of Bake-Off recipes in which a finalist took an eligible product and turned it into something else. But this is by no means the only way home cooks have gotten into the Contest; plenty of people have become finalists by using pizza dough to make pizza, or cookie dough to make cookies. (Since 1968, at least some refrigerated dough products have been eligible ingredients in each Pillsbury Bake-Off Contest. General Mills owns the Pillsbury refrigerated dough products and the Pillsbury Bake-Off Contest, and it licenses the Pillsbury brand to Smucker's for certain shelf-stable baking products, including brownie mixes and canned frosting. The brownie mixes and frosting have not been consistently eligible ingredients in the Pillsbury Bake-Off Contest.)

The numbers in parentheses are the competition numbers. Most of these recipes appear on pillsbury.com.

BAKE-OFF RECIPES THAT REPURPOSED PILLSBURY PRODUCTS

Pillsbury or Pillsbury Grands! Refrigerated Biscuits

Asian Chicken Steam Buns Over Vegetables by Jen Beckman (#46)
Baked Pork Chops With Biscuit Stuffin' by Marion Ohl (#22)
Blueberry-Almond Crème Muffins by Cynthia Bowser (#44)
Carnitas Gorditas With Creamy Chipotle Sauce by Holly Melville (#47)
Cherry Almond Kolache Bake by Barbara Catlin Craven (#46)
Chick-n-Broccoli Pot Pies by Linda Wood (#28) GRAND-PRIZE WINNER
Chicken and Bacon Peppadew Pepper Paninis by Donna Beck (#47)
Chicken and Spinach Biscuit Gyros by Bethany Perry (#46)
Chili-Coconut Shrimp Tacos by Kalani Allred (#47)
Chinese Roast Pork Buns by Wayne Hu (#36)
Chorizo Potato Puffy Tacos by Melissa Stadler (#46)
Coconut-Almond Doughnut Pop-ems by Kathy Matulewicz (#45)
Country Apple Coffee Cake by Susan Porubcan (#31) GRAND-PRIZE WINNER
Country Blueberry Coffee Cake by Wendy L. Hart (#38)
Double-Stacked Pupusas With Curtido Slaw by Lori McLain (#47)
Easy Asian Pork Bundles by Tomoko Long (#47)
Easy Caprese Pizza Bake by Sheila Suhan (#46)
Espresso Hazelnut Beignets by Karyn Hentz (#46)
German Chocolate Doughnuts by Lise Sullivan Ode (#46). See profile, page 104
Grizzly Bear Claws by Gerald Martinez (#47)
Jalapeño Cheddar Waffle Melts by Brenda Washnock (#47)
Lemon-Pecan Sunburst Coffee Cake by Jennifer Peterson (#38)
Lemon–Poppy Seed Pull-Apart Bread by Cathy Wiechert (#47). See profile, page 72
Naan Greek Pizza by Wendi Wallerstein (#46)
Navajo Chicken Tostadas by Sindee Morgan (#47). See profile, page 108
Orange Cream Bomboloni by Toni Dishman (#46)
Pastrami-Pretzel Bites by Laura Stanke (#47)
Peppered Bacon-Wrapped Turkey Pub Sandwiches by Betty Staufenbiel (#47)
Quick Cheese Coffee Cake by Johanna Yoakum (#30)
Raspberry-Filled Jelly Doughnuts by Ted Viveiros (#34)

BAKE-OFF RECIPES THAT REPURPOSED PILLSBURY PRODUCTS

Red White and Blue Dessert Tacos by Charlotte Giltner (#46)
Sausage-Stuffed Waffles With Blackberry Sauce by Sherry Ricci (#46)
Shrimp Salad Pita-Wiches by Beth Royals (#41). *See* profile, page 126
Zesty Lime-Fish Tacos by Kellie White (#44). *See* profile, page 95

Pillsbury Refrigerated Cookie Dough

Blueberry Muffin Tops by Susan Spicko (#44)
Blueberry Sour Cream Pancakes by Michele Kusma (#46). *See* profile, page 47
Brown Sugar–Topped Chocolate Swirl Coffee Cake by Ronald Grasgreen (#46)
Caprese Corn Cakes by Mary Beth Protomastro (#47). *See* introduction, page 1
Caramelized Peach Upside-Down Coffee Cake by Brenda Watts (#45).
   See profile, page 55
Chocolate Cherry Soufflé Cupcakes by Brenda Watts (#46). *See* profile, page 55
Cinnamon-Pumpkin Muffins by Anna Zorko (#47)
Glazed Orange Muffins by Paula Mahagnoul (#47)
Heavenly Hazelnut Torte With Mascarpone Cream by Brett Youmans (#46)
Lemon-Blueberry Macadamia Waffles by David Dahlman (#46)
Macaroon–Peanut Butter–Chocolate Tartlets by Brenda Watts (#47).
   See profile, page 55; recipe, page 155
Mini Carrot-Spiced Cupcakes With Molasses Buttercream by Natalie
   Morales (#45)
Mini Ice Cream Cookie Cups by Sue Compton (#44) GRAND-PRIZE WINNER
Nutty Caramel Cookie Tart by Shannon Kohn (#43)
"O My Ganache" Cherry Macaroon Torte by Dennis Deel (#44)
PB&J Mini Walnut Muffins by Anne Johnson (#46)
Peanut Butter Boston Cream Cake by Mary Beth Mandola (#45)
Peanut Butter–Chocolate Chip Waffles by Julee Shapiro (#47)
Pecan Cookie Waffles With Honey-Cinnamon Butter by Cathy Wiechert (#44).
   See profile, page 72
Sausage-Pancake Muffins by Rebecca Fink (#47)
Strawberries and Chocolate Sugar Cookie Crepes by Juliette Smith (#46)

BAKE-OFF RECIPES THAT REPURPOSED PILLSBURY PRODUCTS

Strawberry-Mascarpone-Hazelnut Chocolate Tart by Pamela Shank (#47). *See* profile, page 80

Sugar Cookie Chocolate Crunch Fudge by Dick Boulanger (#42)

Sweet and Salty Cookie Pie by Bobbie Harms (#46)

Pillsbury Refrigerated Breadsticks

Caprese Pesto Margherita Stackers by Julie Beckwith (#44)

Cashew Chicken Twists With Spicy Orange Sauce by Lauren Wyler (#46)

Chile Cheese Puffs by Larry Lowman (#40)

Chocolate-Peanut Butter-Filled Pretzels by Elizabeth Bennett (#47)

Family-Sized Muffuletta by Margaret Scott (#39)

Glazed Bacon Rollups by Linda Blakely (#46)

Meatball and Breadstick Sub Skewers by Kim Van Dunk (#46). *See* profile, page 86

"Peanut Butter-licious" Ring-a-Rounds by Erika Couch (#43)

Pickled & Twisted Spicy Pork Cemitas by Laura Lufkin (#47)

Sesame-Crouton Asian Chicken Salad by Katie Long (#44)

Pillsbury Crescent Rounds, Dinner Rolls, or Dough Sheet

Apricot-Ginger Cheese Danish by Marla Clark (#44)

Asian Scallion Buns With Sweet and Sour Sauce by Nancy Olson (#45)

Cheesy Crescent Nachos by Gregg Peroutka (#31)

Chicken and Cheese Crescent Chimichangas by Marlene Zebleckis (#33)

Chocolate Doughnut Poppers by Megan Beimer (#47)

Crafty Crescent Lasagna by Betty Taylor (#19)

Creamy Corn–Filled Sweet Peppers by Jody Walker (#47)

Crescent Caramel Swirl by Lois Ann Groves (#27) GRAND-PRIZE WINNER

Crescent Oriental Egg Rolls by Judith Wilson Merritt (#32)

Crescent Samosa Sandwiches by Elisabeth Crawford (#36)

Crescent Three-Cheese Calzones by Irene McEwen (#32)

Curry Chicken–Crescent Wontons by Roxanne Gooding (#47)

Easy Crescent Danish Rolls by Barbara S. Gibson (#26) GRAND-PRIZE WINNER

BAKE-OFF RECIPES THAT REPURPOSED PILLSBURY PRODUCTS

French Toast Waffles With Apple Cherry Topping by Tiffany Aaron (#46)

Italian Zucchini Crescent Pie by Millicent (Caplan) Nathan (#29)
  GRAND-PRIZE WINNER

Loaded Potato Pinwheels by Glori Spriggs (#46) **GRAND-PRIZE WINNER**

Magic Marshmallow Crescent Puffs by Edna Walker (#20) **GRAND-PRIZE WINNER**

Mango–Lemon Drop Sunshine Puffs by Amber Schofield (#45)

Peanut Butter Caramel Sticky Rolls by Wendy Wiseman (#46)

Pumpkin Ravioli With Salted Caramel Whipped Cream by Christina Verrelli (#45). *See* profile, page 131 **GRAND-PRIZE WINNER**

Quick and Fruity Crescent Waffles by Renee Heimerl (#43)

Quick Crescent Baklava by Annette Erbeck (#29)

Quick Crescent Pecan Pie Bars by Albina Flieller (#24) **GRAND-PRIZE WINNER**

Raspberry Ripple Crescent Coffee Cake by Priscilla Yee (#32)

Salmon Crescent Sushi Rolls by Julie McIntire (#45)

Southwestern Corn Poppers by Sindee Morgan (#45). *See* profile, page 108

Sugar-Crusted Almond Pastries by Karla Kunoff (#37)

Upside Down Tomato Basil and Chicken Tartlets by Julie Beckwith (#46)

Waffled Pizza Dippers by Patty Knighton (#41)

Pillsbury or Pillsbury Grands! Refrigerated Cinnamon Rolls

Bacon and Date Cinnamon Roll Strata by Rita Hattrup (#47)

Blueberry Cinnamon Roll Coffee Cake by Marie Sheppard (#46). *See* profile, page 10

Chai-Glazed Cinnamon Waffles by Mimi Chang (#47)

Chocolate Hazelnut–Toffee Bread Pudding With Candied Bacon by Lynne Laino (#47)

Cinnamon Roll Cranberry Orange Pull Apart by Leah Stacey (#46)

Cinnamon Roll–Pear Bread Pudding by Elizabeth Albert (#47)

Gooey Caramel Apple Pull-Aparts by Lisa McDaniel (#42)

Macaroon–Cinnamon Roll Braid by Barbara Lento (#47)

Mocha Cappuccino Pull-Apart Coffee Cake by Janet Gill (#46)

Strawberry–Cinnamon Roll Belgian Waffles by Kelly Humphreys (#47)

BAKE-OFF RECIPES THAT REPURPOSED PILLSBURY PRODUCTS

Pillsbury Refrigerated Crusty French Loaf

Apple Pie Breakfast Bake by Debbie Rowe (#46)

Boston Cream French Toast by Kristen Abbott (#46)

Chicken Caprese Focaccia by Nadine Clark (#46)

Chicken Florentine "Gnocchi" by Shana Butler (#47). *See* profile, page 42

Dark Cherry–Chocolate Breakfast Pastry by MaryAnne Salaway (#45)

Glazed Hawaiian Braid by Cindy Nerat (#47)

Golden Fruit Brioche Rolls by Christine Wilson (#47)

Herb Chicken Sliders With Raspberry Mustard by Laureen Pittman (#44). *See* profile, page 76

Spinach Dip–Stuffed Garlic Rolls by Marie Valdes (#47). *See* profile, page 33; recipe, page 154

Tuscan Veggie Strata by Kim Hookman (#46)

Pillsbury Refrigerated Pizza Crust

Bacon, Caesar and Mozzarella Panini by Carole Strachan (#43)

Balsamic Chicken Cranberry Panzanella by Kalani Allred (#46)

Caprese Grilled Cheese Sandwiches by Ann Goncheroski (#47)

Cherry-Orange Pull-Apart Breakfast Bread by Maria Rokas (#47)

Chicken Chipotle Calzones by Mary Bernier (#47)

Chicken Florentine Panini by Denise JoAnne Yennie (#40) **GRAND-PRIZE WINNER**

Citrus-Shrimp Wraps by Sandra Gallant (#45)

Cranberry Orange Dark Chocolate Flatbread by Arlene Erlbach (#46). *See* profile, page 28

Fiesta Baked Tamales by Tom Piantek (#47)

Honey Chicken and Corn Rafts by Marie Valdes (#46). *See* profile, page 33

Honey Sesame Bagels by Kellie White (#46). *See* profile, page 95

Pepper Jack–Salsa Flatbread With an Italian Twist by JoAnn Belack (#47). *See* profile, page 91

Prosciutto-Spinach Spirals by Terri Rapp (#45)

Sausage Apple and Brie Stromboli by Mary Jo Fletcher LaRocco (#46)

Stuffed Onion Packets With Cheese Sauce by Donna Newcomer (#45)

BAKE-OFF RECIPES THAT REPURPOSED PILLSBURY PRODUCTS

Tomato-Topped Onion Bread Wedges by Sandra Bangham (#36)

Veggie Frittata Breakfast Sandwiches by Jon Winkeller (#46)

Zesty Cheese Bread by Barbara Jones (#38)

Pillsbury Refrigerated Pie Crust

Bacon–Peanut Butter Chocolate Fries by Carolyn Nace (#47)

Baked Chorizo Chili Quesadilla by Laura Ware (#46)

Chicken Empanada Cones by Donna Wolfe (#45)

Chocolate-Dipped Peanut Butter Empanadas by Susan Hubickey (#45)

Chocolate-Orange Pastries by Pam Tapia (#44)

Cranberry-Orange Baklava Pinwheels by Carrie Hudkins (#45)

Italian Spinach Torta by Larry Elder (#33)

Lemon Almond Breakfast Pastry by Sharon Richardson (#33)

Mediterranean Chicken Vegetable Galette by Dinah Surh (#46)

Peanutty Pie Crust Clusters by Beth Royals (#47). *See* profile, page 126; recipe, page 156 **GRAND-PRIZE WINNER**

Spicy Beef and Sweet Potato Samosas by Jennifer Fisher (#46)

Swedish Apple Mini-Dumplings by Stella Riley Bender (#36)

Pillsbury Brownie Mix

Almond Brownie–Cherry Mousse Torte by Catherine White (#44)

Brownie Ganache Torte by Barbara Estabrook (#41)

Brownie Macaroons by Ronald Grosgreen (#39)

Brownie Soufflé Cake With Mint Cream by Edwina Gadsby (#38)

Chai Brownie Cupcakes With Creamy Froth by Chris Caston (#44)

Chocolate-Caramel Crumb Cupcakes by Carole Holt (#44)

Chocolate Mousse Fantasy Torte by Christine Vidra (#34)

Cream-Filled Strawberry-Brownie Cake by Doris Wallace (#45)

Fudgy Orange Cappuccino Torte by Sharla Jack (#35)

Molten Mocha Cakes by Janet Barton (#40)

Pistachio Mousse Brownie Torte by Jane Estrin (#43)

Spiced Chocolate Cupcakes With Caramel Buttercream by Lori Falce (#45)

BAKE-OFF RECIPES THAT REPURPOSED PILLSBURY PRODUCTS

Strawberry Swirl–Peanut Butter–Brownie Cupcakes by Amy Siegel (#45). *See* profile, page 99

Thick and Fudgy Triple Chocolate Pudding Cake by Janice Kollar (#39)

Walnut Fudge Bars by Mabel Patent (#39)

Pillsbury Frosting

Coconut Pecan Chocolate Fudge by Lesley Pew (#46). *See* profile, page 114

Coconut Pecan Florentine Sandwich Cookies by Paula Mahagnoul (#46)

Creamy Peanut Butter Truffles by Denny Gross (#46)

Dark Chocolate Orange Mousse by Dion Fischer (#46)

Fudgy Chocolate Hazelnut Bars by Julie Pando (#46)

Hot Pink Raspberry and Cream Cake by Dawn Onuffer (#46)

Malted Milk Ball Peanut Butter Cream Squares by Craig Partin (#46)

Piña Colada Fudge by Michelle Grosella (#40)

Thick and Fudgy Triple Chocolate Pudding Cake by Janice Kollar (#39)

Toffee Mocha Velvet by Persis Schlosser (#39)

APPENDIX C

Three Award-Winning Recipes From the 47th Pillsbury Bake-Off Contest

THREE AWARD-WINNING RECIPES

Spinach Dip-Stuffed Garlic Rolls

CLEVER TWIST AWARD

Marie Valdes (see page 33)

½ cup butter, melted
1 tablespoon Watkins Garlic Powder
⅔ cup grated Parmesan cheese
1 box (9 oz) frozen chopped spinach
4 oz (half of 8-oz package) cream cheese, softened
1 tablespoon Worcestershire sauce
1 can Pillsbury refrigerated crusty French loaf

1. Heat oven to 350°F. Spray 12 regular-size muffin cups with Crisco Original No-Stick Cooking Spray. Spoon 1 teaspoon of the melted butter into each muffin cup. Sprinkle ⅛ teaspoon of the garlic powder and 1 teaspoon of the Parmesan cheese into each muffin cup.

2. Microwave frozen spinach as directed on box 3 to 4 minutes to thaw. Drain well; squeeze dry with paper towels. In small bowl, mix spinach, cream cheese, 1 teaspoon of the garlic powder, ⅓ cup of the Parmesan cheese, and the Worcestershire sauce until blended. Shape mixture into 12 (1½-inch) balls.

3. Remove dough from can; cut into 12 equal slices. Press each to form 3-inch round. Place 1 spinach ball in center of each dough round. Carefully wrap dough around ball; pinch edges to seal completely. Place seam side down in muffin cups.

4. Bake 17 to 25 minutes or until golden brown. Cool in pan 2 minutes. Loosen with tip of knife. Remove from pan; place on serving platter. Brush each roll with remaining melted butter; sprinkle with remaining garlic powder and Parmesan cheese. Serve warm.

SERVINGS: 12

THREE AWARD-WINNING RECIPES

Macaroon-Peanut Butter-Chocolate Tartlets

JIF PEANUT BUTTER AWARD

Brenda Watts (see page 55)

2 cups flaked coconut	¾ cup powdered sugar
1 roll Pillsbury refrigerated peanut butter cookie dough	1½ teaspoons Watkins Coconut Extract
2 containers (8 oz each) mascarpone cheese	1 cup Jif Whips Whipped Peanut Butter and Chocolate Flavored Spread

1. Heat oven to 350°F. Place Reynolds Foil Baking Cups in 20 regular-size muffin cups. Line cookie sheet with Reynolds Parchment Paper. Spread ½ cup of the coconut on cookie sheet. Bake 5 to 7 minutes, stirring occasionally, until golden brown. Remove to plate to cool.

2. In shallow bowl, place remaining 1½ cups coconut. Shape cookie dough into 20 (1½-inch) balls. Roll each ball in coconut, pressing coconut lightly into dough. With floured fingers, press balls in bottom and halfway up sides of muffin cups. Bake 10 to 16 minutes or until golden brown. Cool 3 minutes; remove from pans to cooling racks. Cool completely, about 15 minutes. Remove foil baking cups.

3. In small bowl, beat 4 oz (½ cup) of the mascarpone cheese, ¼ cup of the powdered sugar, and ½ teaspoon of the coconut extract with whisk until smooth; set aside.

4. In large bowl, beat remaining 12 oz (1½ cups) mascarpone cheese, the chocolate spread, remaining ½ cup powdered sugar, and remaining 1 teaspoon coconut extract with electric mixer on medium speed 1 to 2 minutes or until smooth. Spoon about 2 tablespoons chocolate mixture into each cookie cup. Top with 1 teaspoon mascarpone mixture; sprinkle with toasted coconut. Store covered in refrigerator.

SERVINGS: 20

THREE AWARD-WINNING RECIPES

Peanutty Pie Crust Clusters

GRAND PRIZE

Beth Royals (see page 126)

- 1 Pillsbury refrigerated pie crust, softened as directed on box
- 1 bag (12 oz) white vanilla baking chips (2 cups)
- 1 tablespoon Crisco Baking Sticks Butter Flavor All-Vegetable Shortening
- 1 tablespoon Jif Creamy Peanut Butter
- 1 cup salted cocktail peanuts
- ⅔ cup toffee bits

1. Heat oven to 450°F. Line 2 cookie sheets with Reynolds Cut-Rite Wax Paper.

2. Unroll pie crust on work surface. With pizza cutter or knife, cut into 16 rows by 16 rows to make small squares. Arrange squares in single layer on large ungreased cookie sheet. Bake 6 to 8 minutes or until light golden brown. Remove squares from pan to cooling rack. Cool completely, about 5 minutes.

3. In large microwavable bowl, microwave baking chips, shortening, and peanut butter uncovered on High 1 minute to 1 minute 30 seconds, stirring once, until chips can be stirred smooth. Add pie crust squares, peanuts, and toffee bits; stir gently until evenly coated. Immediately drop by heaping tablespoonfuls onto lined cookie sheets. (If mixture gets too thick, microwave on High 15 seconds; stir.) Refrigerate about 15 minutes or until set. Store covered.

SERVINGS: 30

APPENDIX D

Further Reading

Baked-Off! Memoirs of a Pillsbury Bake-Off Junkie by Steve Grieger (Xlibris, 2009)
Cookoff: Recipe Fever in America by Amy Sutherland (Penguin Group, 2003)
Pillsbury Bake-Off® Winning Recipes (Rodale, 2015)
Pillsbury Best of the Bake-Off® Cookbook (Clarkson Potter, 1996, 2001)
The Ungarnished Truth: A Cooking Contest Memoir by Ellie Mathews (Berkley Publishing Group, 2008)

Blogs by Pillsbury Bake-Off Finalists Profiled in *Smart Cookies*

BakingBrenda (bakingbrenda.blogspot.com) by Brenda Watts, page 55
Cookie Madness (cookiemadness.net) by Anna Ginsberg, page 135
Cybercook's Cooking Corner (cybercookscookingcorner.blogspot.com) by Carole Resnick, page 51
The Dutch Baker's Daughter (thedutchbakersdaughter.com) by Cathy Wiechert, page 72
Epicuricloud (epicuricloud.com) by Christina Verrelli, page 131
The Gluten-Free Maven (theglutenfreemaven.com) by Amy Siegel, page 99
Grandma Honey's House (grandmahoneyshouse.com) by Pamela Shank, page 80
Life in the Van (lifeinthevan.com) by Kim Van Dunk, page 86
Mom Loves Baking (momlovesbaking.com) by Lise Sullivan Ode, page 104

Index

America's Best Cook, 133
America's Test Kitchen, 12
Ask Chef Dennis: A Culinary Journey, 53
Atkins, Jann, 127
Austin (Texas) *American-Statesman*, 135
Baked Chicken and Spinach Stuffing, 28, 135–140
BakingBrenda, 56
Banana Chocolate Brunch Cake, 14–17
Banana–Chocolate Chip Streusel Muffins, 86–90
Banana Crunch Cake, 72
Barefoot Contessa, 24, 97
Behar, Joy, 7, 61
Belack, JoAnn, 67, 85, 91–94
Bergen (N.J.) *Record*, 1
Best of the Bake-Off, 62
Better Homes and Gardens, 24, 89, 133
Bickta, Susan, 65
Black-Bottomed Brandy Bites, 31
Blueberry Cinnamon Roll Coffee Cake, 10–13
Blueberry Sour Cream Pancakes, 3, 47–50, 106
Bon Appétit, 12, 57, 97, 102
Broccoli-Cauliflower Tetrazzini, 7
Brown, Alton, 21
Bruno, Marie, 3, 9, 22–25, 64
Butler, Shana, 41, 42–46, 66
Buttered Rum Fudge, 114
Caprese Corn Cakes, 3
Caramelized Peach Upside-Down Coffee Cake, 55–59
Caramel Nut Bars, 137
Carrot Cupcakes With Coconut Pecan Frosting, 18–21
Cheesy Cauliflower Tartlets, 76–79
The Chew, 39, 127
Chewy Ginger Date Granola Bars, 91
Chewy Gingersnaps With White Chocolate Drizzle, 47–50
Chicken Florentine "Gnocchi," 42–46

INDEX

Child, Julia, 116, 120
Chocolate Cherry Bars, 72, 106
Chocolate Cherry Soufflé Cupcakes, 3, 55–59
Chocolate Doughnut Poppers, 30, 127
Chocolate Hazelnut Torte, 2, 3
Chocolate Praline Layer Cake, 106
Chopped, 21, 97, 102
Chorizo Party Appetizers, 37–40
Christmas Molasses Biscotti, 23
Cinco de Mayo Glazed Chicken Wings, 60–63
Claiborne, Craig, 120
The Columbus (Ohio) *Dispatch*, 48
Coconut-Almond Doughnut Pop-ems, 1
Coconut Pecan Chocolate Fudge, 114–117
Compton, Sue, 96, 119
Cookie Madness, 137
Cooking Contest Central, 76, 93
Cooking Light, 138
Cookoff: Recipe Fever in America, 93
Cook's Country (magazine), 89, 102
Cook's Country (TV show), 12
Cook's Illustrated, 12, 88, 97, 133
Country Living, 61
Country Woman, 89
Cranberry Orange Dark Chocolate Flatbread, 28–32
Creamy Corn–Filled Sweet Peppers, 30, 127
Creamy Lemon-Poppyseed Tart, 16

Croce, Victoria, 21, 27, 37–40, 65
Cuban-Style Sandwich Pockets, 30, 127
Cuisine at Home, 133
Cupcake Wars, 19, 102
Cybercook's Cooking Corner, 52
The Daily Cookie: 365 Tempting Treats for the Sweetest Year of Your Life, 137
Decadent Chocolate Hazelnut Tart, 3, 22–25
Deen, Paula, 82
De Laurentiis, Giada, 120
Double-Delight Peanut Butter Cookies, 81
Double-Layer Mint Fudge, 114
Drumm, Linda, 41, 60–63
The Dutch Baker's Daughter, 75
EatingWell, 83, 88, 138
Epicuricloud, 133
Erlbach, Arlene, 27, 28–32, 65
Family Circle, 83, 138
Festive Eggnog Cake, 102
Flay, Bobby, 43, 120
FoodGal, 131
Food Network, 43, 62, 76, 79, 82, 97, 110, 124, 133, 138
Food Network Magazine, 30, 82, 138
Food & Wine, 94, 120, 138
French Silk Chocolate Pie, 7, 86
Fudgy Bonbons, 106
Garten, Ina, 24, 120
German Chocolate Doughnuts, 3, 104–107

INDEX

Ginsberg, Anna, 28, 70, 125, 135–140
Givler, Heidi, 9, 18–21, 64
The Gluten-Free Maven, 100
Gluten Free & More, 102
Good Housekeeping, 10, 89
Gourmet, 116
Grandma Honey's House, 83
Gurtz, Carolyn, 81
Ham and Cheese Crescent Snacks, 7
Hawkes, Mary, 9, 14–17, 64
Hazan, Marcella, 120
Herb Chicken Sliders With Raspberry Mustard, 76–79
Hirschy, Henry, 130
Holmberg, Martha, 135
Honey Chicken and Corn Rafts, 33–36
Honey Sesame Bagels, 95–98
Hot and Hearty Heroes, 14–17
Houston Chronicle, 128
Hubachek, Hank, 76
Italian Brunch Strata, 91
Jalapeño Cheddar Muffins With Peach Filling, 100
Jung, Carolyn, 131
The Kids' Business Book, 31
The Kitchen, 124
Kusma, Michele, 3, 41, 47–50, 65, 66, 106
Lagasse, Emeril, 76
Lakshmi, Padma, 7
Lee, Sandra, 81
Lemon-Blueberry Muffins, 104–107
Lemon-Broccoli Risotto Rounds, 10–13
Lemon–Poppy Seed Pull-Apart Bread, 72–75
The Lies That Bind, 78
Life in the Van, 87
Loaded Potato Pinwheels, 88
Long Island (N.Y.) *Newsday*, 102
Macadamia Fudge Torte, 73
Macaroon–Peanut Butter–Chocolate Tartlets, 55–59
Magic Marshmallow Crescent Puffs, 6
"Mamma Mia" Ravioli Bites, 91–94
Martha Stewart Living, 107
Marvelous Mediterranean Falafel Sliders, 102
Mascarpone-Filled Cranberry-Walnut Rolls, 80–83
MasterChef, 110
Matulewicz, Kathy, 1
McNamara, Helen Mae, 55–59
Meatball and Breadstick Sub Skewers, 3, 86–90
Mediterranean Sandwich Pockets, 14–17
Melissa's Southern Style Kitchen, 53
Mexican Egg Salad Wraps, 51–54
Miller, Robin, 138
Mini Ice Cream Cookie Cups, 96, 119
Mom Loves Baking, 105–107, 128
More, 4
Morgan, Sindee, 65, 69, 85, 108–111

INDEX

Muffuletta Quiche Cups, 118–121
Nanny's Full o' Love Glazed Carrot Cake, 61
National Enquirer, 105
Navajo Chicken Tostadas, 108–111
Neidlinger, Cherylanne, 21
Newman, Paul, 10
New Orleans Andouille Shrimp Pizza, 37–40
Nick Jr., 128
Noble Pig, 53
Ode, Lise Sullivan, 3, 64, 68, 85, 104–107, 128
Off the Hook on the Plate, 53
The Oprah Winfrey Show, 95, 135
Orange Cardamom Blueberry Crostata, 72–75
Organic Gardening, 89
Osmond, Marie, 7
Pancetta Pear and Pecan Puffs, 31
Peachy Cream Cheese Appetizers, 42–46
Peanut Blossoms, 7
Peanut Browned Butter Banana-Bacon Cookies, 137
Peanut Butter Crunch Layer Bars, 122–124
Peanut Butter–Toffee Cheesecake Brownies, 80–83
Peanutty Pie Crust Clusters, 30, 106, 126–130

Pecan Cookie Waffles With Honey-Cinnamon Butter, 72–75
Pepper Jack–Salsa Flatbread With an Italian Twist, 91–94
Pew, Lesley, 68, 113, 114–117
Pifer, Becky, 69, 113, 122–124
Pittman, Laureen, 5, 67, 71, 76–79
Potts, Victoria. *See* Croce, Victoria
Presley, Elvis, 137
Pudwill, Elizabeth, 128
Pumpkin Ravioli With Salted Caramel Whipped Cream, 2, 131–134
Pumpkin Snowballs, 73
Rachael Ray Every Day, 30
Ramsay, Gordon, 102
Reagan, Ronald, 7
Real Simple, 138
Resnick, Carole, 41, 51–54
Rhubarb Crumb Cake, 75
Rollings, Kim, 70, 113, 118–121
Romper Room, 72
Roosevelt, Eleanor, 7
Royals, Beth, 70, 79, 125, 126–130
San Diego Living, 43
The San Diego Union-Tribune, 43
Saveur, 94, 97, 120
Savory and Sweet Breakfast Biscuit Sliders, 131–134
Sesame Mini Pitas With Roasted Red Pepper Tapenade, 4, 99–103
Sesame Street, 138
Shank, Pamela, 67, 71, 80–83

INDEX

Sheppard, Marie, 9, 10–13
Shrimp Salad Pita-Wiches, 126–130
Siegel, Amy, 1–5, 65, 85, 99–103
Simple Peanut Butter Fudge, 114
Smoky Onion-Custard Tarts, 28–32
Snappy Turtle Cookies, 106
Southwestern Corn Poppers, 108–111
Spicy Apple Twists, 106
Spicy Barbecue Triangles With Raita, 135–140
Spinach Dip–Stuffed Garlic Rolls, 33–36
Spinach, Turkey, and Apple Salad, 10
Spriggs, Glori, 88
Stewart, Martha, 2, 132
Stone, Connie, 16
Strawberry Birthday Cake, 102
Strawberry-Mascarpone-Hazelnut Chocolate Tart, 80–83
Strawberry Swirl–Peanut Butter–Brownie Cupcakes, 1, 99–103
Sutherland, Amy, 93
Sweet and Salty Chocolate Chip–Maple–Peanut Bars, 28–32
Tampa Tribune, 35
Taste of Home, 30, 31, 89, 107
Texas Co-op Power, 139
Top Chef, 138
Tunnel of Fudge Cake, 7, 86
Ultimate Recipe Showdown, 79
Upside-Down Caramel-Apple Biscuits, 76–79
Valdes, Marie, 27, 33–36, 65
Van Dunk, Kim, 3, 4, 65, 85, 86–90
Vermont Maple Bread Pudding, 126–130
Verrelli, Christina, 2, 125, 131–134
Watts, Brenda, 3, 41, 55–59, 66
White, Kellie, 68, 85, 95–98
Wiechert, Cathy, 67, 71, 72–75
Will Cook for Smiles, 53
Winfrey, Oprah, 135
Yearwood, Trisha, 82
Zesty Lime-Fish Tacos, 95–98

www.ingramcontent.com/pod-product-compliance
Lightning Source LLC
Chambersburg PA
CBHW070618300426
44113CB00010B/1574